The Furies
and
The Flame

Ingrid Rimland

a true story

Arena Press
a division of ATP
20 Commercial Blvd.
Novato, California 94947

FIRST EDITION

Library of Congress Cataloging in Progress
ISBN: 0-87879-418-2

84 85 86 87 88 10 9 8 7 6 5 4 3 2 1

To my children,

Erwin and Rudy,

with love and respect

Contents

U.S.A.

Paraguay

CHAPTER ONE

Five Seconds

M Y FRIENDS WOULD CRY, aghast, once it was known
that my Mennonite marriage had shattered:
"But you loved him! Didn't you love him?"

Ah, yes. So I did. What can I say? Love drew me like a pied piper. But then there was a child.

Here is Erwin's story—and mine. Here is the road we were destined to travel, mother and son, linked by an accident of circumstance, the whimsy of romantic folly, and those chains of love and kin and heritage that turned into the shackled armor from which I fought my pious world.

Two decades lie within me like a giant psychic wound, but before me, for five seconds, I see glory.

Or do I?

Who is to say?

Let this be known: it was a ghoulish thing to happen to a baby. Don't cheapen grief by telling me it was God's will—how could that be? Don't say it was my cross to bear—I did not choose it. Don't tell me in smug ignorance that in the end his tragedy was meant to strengthen me—life's balances can't be that simple. Don't tell me that Erwin is happy, well-liked, productive, that he has an excellent memory, the diligence and perseverance of an ant, the heart and soul of an angel, and more friends than you and I. I know all that—I fought for it. Is it enough? Forever will I mourn the child that should have been. Forever.

I know myself. In the mirror of my soul I see myself: a young unworldly girl struck down by unleashed fury—for what? Because I wore red lipstick once? Because I cut my skirts two inches short? Because I read forbidden novels? They say: for my impatient tongue God gave me this burden, to teach me a lesson or two. I listen: not always with grace, not always with patience, not always with calm and composure and quiet forbearance, but always with a writer's inner knowledge that one day there must come a reckoning.

Where is the key?

To this day, I haven't found it, but in my hands I hold five precious seconds. If anything, I traded this: that in the end, it was given to me, to my fervor and fury, to challenge God's merciless hand, to harness what nobody else believed could be harnessed: the steady, strong, relentless courage that rests in the weakest of bodies, the feeblest of minds.

Like Abraham, I wrestled with God for my son.

Take a map, and pick the prickliest, swampiest, muggiest of all jungles, place your finger on a waste and wanton land, and say: "Right here! That's Paraguay." That's where I spent my teenage years.

My people said that we were pacifists, desiring nothing more than peace to till the soil—that a history of bitter persecution, four bloody centuries long, accounted for our strange unworldly ways. From the Fiend's very teeth we had managed to escape from our persecuted German villages in Russia in a mad, mad scramble for our lives in the last burning days of an unwholesome war. Look into any face of yesterday and see engraved a past replete with brutal pain.

"Not one of us—not one!—has been spared the slaughter of loved ones, the bite of hunger and cold, the uncounted hardships of years on the road," my granny used to say.

Heartbreaking distances stretched out behind us. Stalin had tried to entomb us, and had succeeded with our men. Then Hitler took the boys still left, put them in uniform, and marked them thus for death. And in the end, the continent that we had known and loved fell to the dust and ashes of warriors' folly and what was left, it seemed, was this: a handful of unbidden women and children whom no one was willing to shelter except a dishevelled land.

A Dutch passenger ship helped us master the waves of the sea. A smaller boat took us upstream. The very last stretch of our journey we travelled in ox carts, creaking and groaning over the uneven land, rawhide roofs stretched tight over framework the shape of half-loops. It's still in the archives, this voyage — now almost forgotten, for years travel fast.

I was then a child of twelve. I remember it sharply: how the animals' skins steamed from the heat, how their flanks, their backs, their ears lay siege to virulent clouds of mosquitos as we moved, cart after cart, deeper and deeper into the tropical bush. A thousand long miles from the sea, with no roads to break the uninhabited waste, no wells to yield a drink, no schools to teach a hungry child, no outside links of any kind to wicked worldly influence, we saw only this and beheld it: vast stretches of new, virgin, pioneer land. In those years, allegiance to the Mennonites was still inherited, not sought, but having been born to The Creed was but a provisional ticket to Heaven — it had to be earned and paid for in good, solid, diligent Mennonite coin.

We built our huts of mud plastered over a wicker frame. We thatched them with the reeds that grew in isolated patches near the camp. We smoothed the bug-infested jungle floor with a mixture of *manioc* and manure and swept it twice a day. We baked our bread in ant hills and cooked our food in tin cans in a ditch.

Proudly, we planted geraniums and roses.

And all the while the Paraguayan jungle belched on us its fetid musky odor. Plant parasites reached out from the trees to detain us, and we would have to duck repeatedly to save ourselves from all the influences alien to our souls. A chorus of insects would whine around us at night in the thickets, and our assaulted blood would crawl. For we, though having lived in the Ukraine for more than fifteen decades and barely knew a Germany at all, still sang our German songs, still said our German prayers, affirmed our German heritage and ancestry, and never thought that strange.

Yes, we were isolationists and pacifists, but had we not been pacifists, I am quite sure we would have punished sloth with death. How, otherwise, could we have persevered in such a choking, broiling, thriving pit? For here we were, some sixteen villages wrought out of a green hell by women and children, cut off from the world by design and default, amid an alien territory where, to plant a tree, ten must be axed, or so a book we shared proclaimed, where ants were as large as the joints of one's fingers, and you could hear them as they cut a swath across the land.

Mail sent by Mennonites from North America came once a month, and often did not come at all. Our richer brethren fed us in the early days—they paid for sugar, rice, and tea. They shipped their cast-off clothing. They sent us rusty jungle knives and prayers and advice. In time we freed ourselves, at least in part. We grew watermelons, *kaffir,* oranges, *manioc*—a starchy root that grows without care, the staple food of Paraguay, believed to make the natives lazy but spurs a Mennonite to stronger feats. We would boil it for hours and place it between us as we toiled at the rim of the bush, dip pieces into heaps of salt we kept on fleshy leaves, and wash it down with sandy, lukewarm water.

"We have duties," we would say.

These were the duties we beheld: cutting roads into the jungle, chopping down gigantic trees, unearthing twisted roots, plowing camps, hoeing fields, digging wells, carting water from depressions in the soil. We raised long-snouted pigs and papayas the size of a football—and the tamest, gentlest children you could find—all in the blistering, murderous heat of a summer that lasted ten months of the year. Even when it poured in buckets on swollen summer days, there was really no relief—only minutes afterwards the sun would lap all moisture from large puddles.

We were the coming jungle generation, just old enough to have been born, just young enough to have escaped the slaughter of its males. My teenage decade was the first that had a boy for every girl.

Was it the furnace-like sun that ripened us early as we set out to tame the bush? Was it the darkness of tropical night that came like a bolt as soon as the sun fell into its vast bed of green? Was it a teenager's thirst for immersion that set me on a path not of my choosing, a path that left no room for reflection at all?

Woldi was mine from the moment I saw him.

He was so agreeable all of the time, such a good and engaging young boy, the comfort of his widowed mother, dependable, hard-working. He had teeth like polished pearls, a smile to be envied in a world devoid of nutrients and vitamins. He was not as shy and unpolished as other playmates from whose ranks I could have chosen, had "choice" entered my fogged-over feelings at all. He was smashing on a horse. He was tan-skinned and black-haired where others were freckled and red. He beheld my face with warm brown eyes where everybody else's eyes, including mine, were blue and had been blue for centuries. He was fine-boned and slender and limber of gait in the black, polished boots he always wore when courting, compared to boys with heavy bones and large, unwashed, bare feet. I see him still. In my innocent vision of youth he was special.

I shanghaied him.

Woldi was a solid Mennonite, for they themselves proclaimed him one—although a technical argument could have been made refuting this perception. My father had been German Lutheran, and his, so rumor had it in those days, came from a distant Jewish family. Not that it mattered: Stalin had taken them both and starved them to death, we assumed. We did not miss them much in our hardened nonchalance of youth. A father was an almost unknown luxury. You do not miss the luxuries you never even knew.

Woldi rolled Low German diphthongs with relish on his tongue, while I, regrettably, was neither fish nor fowl, thanks to a progressive mother who had dipped my tongue in vanity. My mother, Ljuba, was a well-known heretic. Perhaps it was her sinful smoking that set us apart, for it prevented the elders from letting her teach, though she was clearly the best and the brightest young teacher of language they had, and the villages needed her badly. And since she could not teach and must pay her keep in kind if not coin, she was ordered to work as a midwife—work she detested but did admirably well. In her youth in Russia, she had gone to school in Odessa, and it had spoiled her for the faith. She insisted with the fervor of a zealot that I speak High German at all times. My flawless diction, it turned out, remained my mother's deepest lifelong joy. I saw it as my albatross. It made me different. I was too smart, the elders said. For my own good, I needed trimming.

Yes, I was smart, I was strong, I was willful, and I spoke my mind even then, though never too loudly—not then! I knew I was bright as a matter of fact. I couldn't help knowing. No one in our makeshift jungle school of early years was faster with answers than I. But in my flashing, somersaulting mind I did not take much pride—I learned to hide the heady thoughts like other secret vices that sorely jeopardized Heaven: dancing, playing dominoes for orange pits, reading books on weekdays. Being smart was dangerous. I hid my mind the way a well-known thief might hide a treasure of his own, for fear of being suspect.

My life among the Mennonites felt like a fortress from the start, for ours was a God who had commanded His disciples to nip all vanity right in the bud, and therefore all the elders always nipped at me.

People ask: Why?

What can I say? I do not know. Strangely and mysteriously, salvation in my family had skipped two generations — first Mama and then me.

I had no room to breathe, said I.

"I understand," said Ljuba, my pretty, obstinate mother, curling the tips of my braids.

I felt crippled by small minds, by small rules and regulations, I proclaimed.

Mama said: Yes, so did she.

Stale prayers, I told her, did harm to my dreams. Mama looked at me most thoughtfully and lit another cigarette in reprisal. But Oma, my granny, insisted in flattest Low German: *"Je jeleada, je fetjeada."* The more you want, the less you have. The more you stretch, the more twisted you grow. Oma was our cherished matriarch.

That's how I grew up, with a boiling ferment within me, a prickly, alien creature, my prayers unsaid even then. I grew up among those silent, disapproving people, a child so hungry for substance and challenge that I attempted at one point to memorize the Bible backwards so as to stand apart by a simple feat of will. I did this, sitting on a tree stump, the Bible on my sweaty knees, for in our paltry jungle beginnings we had no buildings to speak of, no blackboards, no pencils, no pens. Only of Bibles was there no dearth — our brethren in the North had wisely supplied them. And given these facts of impoverished pioneer living, to this day it is a mystery to me why, in the end, I did not convert to that pitiless zeal that serves a fervent mind so well — what with my need for abandon, my need for words to run like fire through my veins.

Was it any wonder, then, that the handsomest boy within a radius of three hundred miles stood in the path of my impatient youth?

There he stood, young and bronze and ever-so-seductive, beneath a giant tree. He claimed in later years that it was just a common, ant-infested tree, but that's not what my memory tells me. It was a grand and gorgeous tree, high and glossy, a cathedral, and there, beneath its branches, stood a boy, slingshot draped around his wrists, ordained by all the fates for me. He turned. He smiled. A run-of-the-mill Mennonite boy would have shuffled, would have squirmed at the sight of so pretty and daring a girl. I wore freshly ironed ribbons braided artfully throughout my hair, and he clearly liked my long, thick tresses, for he gently touched their tips and gave them a quick, teasing tug: "My . . . my . . ." said he, grown tall and almost a man, " . . . aren't you sassy today . . ."

Of such words are love songs made.

As bliss wore thin in later years he would insist that I had spindly arms and knobby knees. Oh, the treachery of men, unable to behold such moment! My moment by that tree was sheerest sorcery.

I was fourteen. I fell in love. I literally plummeted. It seems to me that in the coming years I fell and fell and fell.

Such are life's careless ways. Perhaps one day my younger son will marry and have children of his own based on an incidental, random moment. I don't know on what haphazard tenets posterity rides. What mill could yield such grist for such long, trying times? For I must acknowledge even now that I loved that boy I first saw by that tree more deeply, more blindly, and with more irrationality than I have ever loved again.

More puzzling still—he did not share my feelings.

It used to astound me. How could he be calm in the face of my need? Why did my sense of wonderment not catch him like a leaping flame?

Not that another girl stood in the way — that might have been an explanation. But no — there were no doubts. I let it be known, loudly and clearly, that I had staked him out as my own. I had declared him mine, and he, good-natured and vaguely pleased, did not at all disagree. As I grew up and for a while worked in a Spanish-speaking city, rumors reached my ears that he had found another post on which to hitch his horse in Village Number Two. I packed my bags in haste and came zipping home to set matters straight then and there.

I put both hands around him and proclaimed him mine for all the world to see. My mother said disdainfully: "Just look at him. He looks like a gypsy." That added fuel to the fire.

She did not know, as I did all too well: it was the other way around. The stranger, the gypsy was me. Woldi, it turned out, was not so sure at all about the merits of a girl who spoke to dogs and chickens in High German. Let's just say my darling took his time. But what he lacked in speed I rounded out with a determined single-mindedness of purpose. The day would surely come when I would marry him.

I married him when I was twenty-one — it took me seven years to convince him. Even my enemies had to admit that he, no doubt, by then was very much in love with me. Not that he ever told me. Not in the long years of our courtship. Not in a marriage that was to last some twenty years. I did not find that strange, for ours was a world of pride and prudery where words were watched as carefully as deeds. But what of that? He held my hand in broiling daylight. He kissed me, full of terror and enchantment, in the dark beneath the *paraiso* trees. All around me, wherever I went, swirled ripples and rapids of gossip. When finally — oh, finally! — he put his hands around my waist and said: " . . . why in the world are we waiting . . . ?" every single tongue and tonguelet started wagging. For gossip had it in those days, maliciously — and incorrectly, by the way! — that in the end, it was a padded bra that clinched it.

CHAPTER TWO

A Legendary Wedding

MORE THAN HALF OF THOSE who axed their way into the wilderness now rest forever in the angry soil of Paraguay. Today, the papers proclaim that the Mennonite jungle colonies flourish, thanks to those first pioneers who pinned their flesh against the thorny bush. In time, loans from the North and assistance from Germany helped. But in those first hot years when money was scarce and harvests a pitiful sight, a tide of doubt swept through the souls of the staunchest of settlers. A struggle unmatched, nowhere recorded, and to what paltry end? "But haven't we given our word . . . ?" someone might say, and someone else would counter: " . . . just think about an iced drink clear of sand and free of ants . . . " Immigration laws had slackened, compared to early post-war years. Shouldn't we pack up and try to join our brethren in the snowy land called Canada?

It was not easy to decide—there were too many pros and cons. Our barefoot life held few rewards. The sun continued to torment. The rains would not loosen, and the crops all but shriveled from the heat. But here lay our future, in a land stretched as far as the eye could absorb, given to us in exchange for a handshake: to be agrarian models, as we had been in Russia, to lesser souls than we.

A life with few rewards, outsiders might have said.

Not so. Not in the least.

It took years of sweat and tears and wasted strength, and even now the struggle is not done. But in good times we counted on our calloused fingers all the things we had achieved: village streets as straight as arrows, prickly fences to keep cattle in and natives out, well-trained dogs to chase away the foxes that fed on our chickens that fed on the insects and weeds of the land so that we, in turn, could feed on the eggs little children tracked down in the thickets. In time, we built a hospital. A five-room school was carefully constructed between the villages named Five and Seven. We drove hand-crafted buggies. We rode horses so carefully brushed that their tails would throw sparks on a Sunday.

And our nights? To that first fierce and much-determined jungle generation who had never known what living " . . . in the wicked world" might be, there was truly ample, magic compensation: nothing could surpass the tropic sheen of moon that rose, yellow and gaudy—twice the size of the moon of Canada!—and started climbing through the trees romantically, while the night with its myriads of glistening stars would stroke and caress our senses. Yes, we were poor, but we were also richly blessed by measures all our own.

That we were destitute by standards of the world when I was wed was not a matter of concern to me. Though one heel had loosened on my only pair of shoes, and Woldi had to swap two frazzled ties for one that he could wear and not stand shamed, we had a wedding that is legend to this day. Ask anybody who attended.

We threw ourselves into a celebration that was to last three days. We barbecued a cow named Isabel, given to us as a generous present by Woldi's older brother, Victor, who was preparing, a traitor, to leave for the North to follow brother Albert, who had married Tina, a girl with Canadian connections, just a few months ago.

"But you will follow, too, won't you . . . !" cried *Mutter*, my mother-in-law-to-be. "We'll file for your papers as soon as we can."

There she was, my newest acquisition, swiftly beheading a fearful number of chickens, explaining tearfully to me, her dubious brand new daughter, the ins and outs of why it was imperative that we must all migrate to Canada. ". . . Why, everyone goes! Albert has already lined up sponsors! You would be the only ones to stay . . . !"

I mixed *manioc* and eggs into gigantic tubs of salad while Woldi kept turning chunks of Isabel on grids to be kept hot for days. I was glad I had a respectable wedding. The milk for the wedding buns came fresh from the households nearby. So did help. So did advice. Scores of neighbors had assembled before dawn from the bridal villages of Seven and Eight. Villages vied with each other for the ostentation and the joy of a wedding on display.

"*Mutter*," I said, choking a little on reluctant familiarity. "I don't think so. We are young. We'll stay here. Let the foolish try their luck in Canada. If Victor wants to leave, he only doubles our property . . . "

"But what will people think!" came *Mutter's* expert battle cry.

What did I care what people thought on this, my happy day? Women, old and young and in-between, arrived in a buzz of eager conversation to commence the scrubbing, sweeping, baking, cooking, broiling tasks that always preceded a wedding. Boys poured through our gates on horseback, sharp machetes slung sideways in their saddles to cut away the adjacent underbrush to make room for long rows of tables and benches. They were a sight to behold, those boys I had grown up with, showing off their riding skills, whirling magnificent creatures, sending clusters of girls screeching in mock horror into the bushes for cover, from where they must be rescued by a flushed and eager knight. Many a budding romance spun off of a wedding, like offshoots from a fallen tree.

We were a generation harboring new values—just look at us and marvel at our spunk: hair brushed sleek behind our ears, soles and knees scrubbed pink, aprons starched to absolute perfection—why should we give a hoot for Canada? Next year, those giggling girls and strutting boys might well be married, too. They would collect the dishes from the neighbors and wind garlands through the roped-together chairs. Flowers—flowers everywhere! Wound through the horses' harness. Draped around the gates through which our guests now poured, around the ostentatious baby chair. "May . . . June . . . July . . . " someone always slyly counted fingers, while I blushed and squirmed and pretended not to hear. Prompt and punctual even at birth, Mennonite babies arrived on the dot—but pity the one who was fast. A lifetime would not be enough to forget such untoward speed.

Yes, a frolicky thing it can be, an authentic Mennonite wedding—even in the worst of circumstances and surroundings it is awesome to behold. Tradition marches mightily at our celebrations. My wedding seemed magnificent beyond compare but also somewhat frightening, partitioning the willfullness of youth from the stern and drab predictability of being married, with the elders stoutly in the middle hardening their rhetoric. We danced at my wedding, believe it or not, dodging the scowls of the vigilant souls, even though we knew they would be busy afterwards for weeks to come tracking down assorted sinners. We danced for two nights, but as the frenzy died down on the third, an elder beckoned us behind an oleander bush and scolded us severely.

I joined my new family and moved into the newer two-room shack we proudly called the Kitchen House—for a kitchen under roof was still an envied luxury. *Mutter* kept the older building. It was crumbling by now and infested with spiders, but *Mutter* said she did not mind—why, with her immigration papers ready . . . Oh, my, not that old song again!

Undaunted, she would chip away at my resistance: "Why,

anyone can go to Canada with a brother willing and able to vouch . . . " Known only from sparse photographs, Canada filled *Mutter* with longings and fears to the brim. She gloried over prospects of push-button gadgets, Kool-Aid drinks in rainbow colors, lacy curtains, well-kept super-roads that could transport, so Albert had assured her, any lonely Mennonite absolutely any time to any distant relative—but what about those glossy magazines, or noisy football matches, or women who drove cars?

I was eager to see her depart.

There was no privacy with *Mutter* underfoot, and I had been, from birth, a solitary soul. She was simply everywhere. And she talked incessantly, and with her thoughts on getting me to Canada, somehow!! that's all I heard all day. When the winter rains came, she moved into our room for comfort and convenient company, as did our two shivering dogs. Winter is short in the tropics, but it chills the marrow in your bones. In the muddy water holes that formed outside our hut, fat frogs would belch and bellow. I hung all the *ponchos* I could find across our open windows. They would flap and dangle in the wind with soggy fringes and only underscore the misery of dreary, dripping days. Brown water seeped through the roof and over the threshold, and the south wall bulged and sagged until one day it collapsed on *Mutter's* bed. I still can hear her wail: " . . . and Albert writes in Caaa-naa-daa . . . "

Thus started married life, in a shivering darkness and irritated state of mind that dulled all my senses and quenched all wanton thoughts. What had I expected? I did not know. Soon I found myself in such a tearful, wretched slump I had no words to name what had befallen me. What had gone wrong? I loved Woldi—was that not true? I clung to him, cold to the roots of my hair, grateful for his hands that stuffed mildewed blankets around me, setting my teeth against the swampy noises of the night: "I love him! I love him! I love him a lot . . . !" Yes, I loved him very much indeed. Of that I was convinced. With all the strength of my passionate twenty-two years.

For years, this thing between us had no name. It took me years to label it, and years again to own up to what such recognition, in the end, must mean.

I think I recognized it first by substance, if not name, when I discovered — much to my shaky surprise — that I was unmistakeably and manifestly pregnant. We had agreed: no babies right away. And now, it seemed, there was one on the way. I said, as a good, seemly Mennonite would: ". . . I believe that I am . . . " letting the meaningful pause speak for itself, for ours was a creed that had no extra words to waste where lowered lashes could be used with expertise to refer to sensitive matters of nature.

I told him by the gate. I always met him by the gate so I could cast it open for his horse and steal my kiss before *Mutter* and dogs would intrude with much noise and frenzy and hullabaloo.

He had put his arms around me, but now he took them back. He hitched his thumbs securely onto the notches of his belt. Thus we stood: he on one side, I on the other, two crudely-hewn two-by-fours, crosswise, between us. I trembled with tension and awe. Day's end, in the jungle, breaks like an extended shriek that sweeps the length and width of consciousness as the sun sinks away, and its final rays fall rapidly through huge *quebracho* trees. It's a disturbing feeling, this insect bedtime hour. It holds discord everywhere. It felt like a nail scratching glass. Like a fool I jumped into words, dropping all pretense, leaning forward eagerly: " . . . I am pregnant . . . " and could have bitten my tongue, for never had I uttered, or so it seemed to me, more unseemly, untoward words.

"What's for supper?" said Woldi.

I thought he had misunderstood.

"I am pregnant," I repeated, like a mule. I could have wept with sorrow for all that might have been.

"You should not talk like that," said Woldi, mildly scolding. Expertly, he snapped at an insect — a last forlorn fly that buzzed around his head. It was a loathsome habit. When something troubled him, when something puzzled him or made him ill-at-ease or left him at a loss for words, he caught himself a buzzing fly. He had one now. He held it, buzzing, to my ears with a small, embarrassed laugh, " . . . listen . . . " as the sun sank away, as the darkness dropped around us.

Woldi did not refer to this awkward matter between us again. Why waste one's words on obvious developments? This shyness between us never abated — in fact, it grew with the years. But as I continued to spread to all sides, and neighbors left and right ceased whispering and started shoving pillows under me, he suddenly discovered a certain budding sense of pride. Why, a celebrity by proxy — that's what he had become!

He announced shyly that he would build me my very own buggy so I could ride around the villages in style. It was clear that he wanted to parade me.

It was a bouncy, two-wheeled delight, light as a breeze, the envy of my neighbors. One day Woldi added: "Now, if you learn to hitch a horse . . . "

"Oh, no," I said. "You are going to take me. To the hospital, I mean. I'm not going into this alone."

"All right," he said, having tried.

He was exceedingly good with his hands. He hammered and painted and polished his loving creation many hours after work and many Sunday mornings while others went to church judgmentally. I would sit nearby, slap at mosquitoes, laugh at his timorous jokes, and fancy myself very lucky. "What about Brunhilde?" I would tease, causing him much agony. "How about Edeltraud, or Waltraud, or Monika?" Vain and fancy names, lifted from some shredded dime novels that kept circulating among those of us who read.

"We could call her Lenchen, you know."

"It will be a boy," I said, quickly. Lena was his mother's name.

Woldi said agreeably: "All right. Though I doubt that it will be a boy."

No, I couldn't complain, I sternly told myself, squashing bugs that crawled about my knees. The clan had departed a few weeks ago. *Mutter,* Victor, Kate, Elsa, Peter, Albert, Tina—everybody gone. Wasn't I lucky? A tried and true husband, all to myself—and not an in-law within sight to interfere—a husband who was running now not only the depleted and delapidated village Number Eight as their duly voted *Schulz* but a sawmill in the bargain, with the help of twenty workers, a few hapless natives, several sets of mulish oxen, and my sage advice. After much coaxing and prodding, he had taken this job. He would have preferred to work in the fields and be inconspicuous. His new position gave us some cash which we sorely needed. But did he like to have to delegate duties to men much older and wiser than he? Only to please me, had he agreed.

CHAPTER THREE

The Perfect Child

WITH WOLDI WORKING at the sawmill, management of our homestead was left solely to me. The work was grueling and hard, but I had strength in abundance. I welcomed strenuous work. It channeled all my energies and made me sweetly tired. I loved getting tired so I could sleep at night. I hoed the weeds in the fields. I chopped the wood I needed for cooking our supper. I scrubbed my sheets to snowy perfection, and to that end I rinsed them twice, even though I had to carry every drop of water the entire length of Number Eight. Every Saturday I swept my yard. I thinned our orange trees. I fed our cattle and horses. I coaxed chickens to hatch in my kitchen and gathered the eggs from the underbrush before the snakes could get to them. These eggs I traded for stamps in the store at Number Five so I could write to Canada.

I wrote many a letter, for I always loved to write. "We don't intend to come to Canada," I wrote defiantly to Albert and Tina and *Mutter*. "We have heady, long-term plans. Three cows have calved, and we have sold a horse . . . "

I wrote those letters with bravado. We had struggled with the jungle now for more than fifteen years. And in the end, it looked as if our colonies might fold. Many had left — one after another. Life was too hard. Only a handful remained, determined to endure the coming decade, come what may. I counted myself stoutly among them — my young impatience in need of A Cause. Ever since I had married and had settled on a homestead of my own, I had bought into the ancient German homestead slogan: *Den Ersten der Tod. Den Zweiten die Not. Den Dritten das Brot.* Death for the first generation. For the second, nothing but hardship. But bread for the third. Limitless land, ours for the asking. So many unclaimed opportunities. If only we could build a road to Asuncion. If only we could buy a boat to start our own exporting. I saw myself, in my assorted reveries, as the first rugged link in a landed dynasty. Though I was sorely vitamin-deficient, though three or four times I just about fainted from heat, though my pregnant body revolted at the greasy, dripping *griebenschmalz* — ground-up residual bacon, the only breakfast spread we could afford — I was sure that I would stay. I would endure. I would be the matriarch in a long, long chain of coming generations. Every Mennonite cell in my blossoming body affirmed it.

It always seemed to me that when a child was born, a village suffered right along, enthusiastically — an event wrought with emotion and elation in which all the living partook. Our first hospital — a thatched-roofed, oblong building where such events took place — lay massively between the villages of Five and Seven. Next to the churches, it was the most revered and awesome place. A stay *"im Krankenhaus"* was akin to rescue, adventure, and honor.

If a woman delivered, you could hear that clearly from the street. She was expected to let it be known that she suffered, for hours and sometimes for days.

"Just wait until it's your turn," my good friend Wera told me with no little malice in her voice. "I've tried it. I know."

I was curious and afraid. When I was a child, and Mama took care of the colony's newborn, I would often linger in the hospital vicinity so I could gather data on mysterious goings-on. She never let me watch, though she would let me listen. I was enchanted by the drama of it all. But I was also wary. Was it pain or was it pomp? Wouldn't you think that such suffering would make a poor mother recline in her pillows, all weak and wan and worn? But no—they simply shone with pride and ostentation only minutes afterwards. Were they faking suffering, just enough to reap some sympathy in a life devoid of tender care? Were they faking happiness so as to minimize the fact that yet another child was born to nothing but mind-killing toil?

Not then, and not since, have I found birth to be the holy miracle it is supposed to be. I wish it had the trappings of a nobler feat, like college graduation—I long for hooded processions and trumpets and drums. I think what really happens looks and feels ridiculous.

In whispers did my married friends reminisce, so as to prepare me. I interrogated Wera at some length. She told me with flushed cheeks:

"It slices you apart with sharp, hot knives. It feels like tongs, believe you me! It rips you, bone to bone . . . "

Therefore, when I began to go into labor, I was surprised how little it hurt. It started so mildly, like a playful jab in my ribs, a teasing cramp that started somewhere deep within me and ended before it began. I chose to ignore it, thinking I had strained a muscle as I bent to yank a hefty plant of *manioc* from the sun-dried, heat-baked ground. I pulled and pulled. Its roots lodged in the jungle soil and, pulling hard, I felt the same sharp cramp again. I thought: "Why, this can't be. For Heaven's sakes, this feels like nothing . . . "

Perplexed, I waddled back into my hut, placed an alarm clock at my feet to time myself, and sat there and waited, a soldier about to go into battle.

What now?

It was still early in the morning. There was no way to reach Woldi with a message; he would not be home until late. Could I hang on? Or should I risk walking all alone through the bush to Number Seven and ask someone I knew—and risk a snicker, surely! — to take me the rest of the way? And what about my buggy — was I to forego my much advertised ride?

I decided to wait. The cramps within me were still underground, though throbbing now, closer in time, and sharp now and then like the point of a needle aimed at my spine.

I waited in my chair all day, sipping *yerba mate*, feeling mildly euphoric by the challenge about to descend upon me. I thought proudly that for all that lore of gore, I was surely doing splendidly.

By evening, Woldi appeared. I reclined with nonchalance. He cast lots of anxious glances. By now, it was pitch-dark outside. I suggested we wait until morning. I felt like a fake, a failure, for suffering so little when all the world had told me I would die.

Woldi said, after a while, his voice very thick: "Shouldn't we better get going . . . ?" I think he was glad for the dark, for his hands shook mightily as he harnessed the horse and hoisted me atop the seat. He must have been quite overwhelmed.

We had a doctor in the villages for serious emergencies, but an ordinary little Mennonite was delivered by a midwife. After my mother ceased to perform that function — for in time the elders relented, permitting her to teach, subject to condition that she smoke — if she must — out of sight in an outhouse, a young girl was appointed to the task. Gredel was barely older than I but of such quiet serenity that doctors and patients trusted her fully. I had counted on Gredel. But she, too, had left for Canada, and now a woman was in charge for whom I had little regard.

It does sound petty now, but I held an old and bearded grudge. I still remembered that one lonely Christmas Eve when I had been a child and she was put in charge of modest Christmas gifts from Canada. She had excluded me — for lack of piety, no doubt. I dreaded her more than I dreaded the pain, but there was no choice — here she was now, glaring at me, no doubt remembering as well, and I her helpless victim! Two days she had spent, she informed me, with a woman from Village Number Six who could not get her child dislodged no matter how she tried. It was, in part, the woman's fault. She was a haughty one—that woman wouldn't yell. "If it hurts, just yell," she instructed me severely. "The more you yell, the faster you'll get done . . . "

Throughout the night I felt like an absolute failure for being so slow and so little in pain, depriving her not only of her sleep but of anticipated drama. "Does it hurt?" she kept asking hopefully, and I kept saying, to spite her: "Oh, no. Not a bit!" It hurt, more and more, but I just longed to lie very still and breathe very deeply and keep my drama to myself like Midas hoarding gold.

"Start walking," she finally ordered. "Every time you feel a pain, start walking back and forth. Get on! Get on!" I hated anyone being so pushy. To walk like a bloated, unwilling hippopotamus in front of this woman who watched me from her chair was sheerest, meanest agony. I wanted her to go away. I was convinced that, on my own, I would do simply splendidly. I remember this night as one of intense psychic discomfort much more than physical pain.

"I'm disgusted with you," she finally said. "Take these two pills. Let's both get some sleep. We'll continue tomorrow."

They made me violently ill, but only seconds afterwards, a giant hand wiped out all pain. I snoozed away until morning. I woke in splendid spirits and woke my glum adversary, slumped sideways in her chair. By then, my pains were sharp and short. I rather enjoyed them as I lay there, savoring the silent last resistance deep within my own sweet cherished privacy of mind.

No, I don't think that Erwin was hurt at his birth—but who is to say? He was a big and strapping boy, lean and long and sturdy. He lay, stirring softly and symmetrically, pink fists pressed against fat cheeks. He seemed a perfect miracle.

We took him home on a cool, very beautiful morning in May, riding slowly and triumphantly the entire length of villages

Seven and Eight. How well I remember this drive of acclaim in our elegant spruced-up buggy. What gorgeous sunshine falling on a gallant, jaunty world. I was pretty. I was young. I was loved. A beautiful son lay asleep in my lap, an absolutely picture-perfect baby. Had I really accomplished this feat — given birth to a new human being? It seemed incredible, and yet it seemed so right. Why, by the flick of his tiny wrist he had already made me his slave!

I would not know another day of happiness like this for more than twenty years.

We put him in a princely crib. I had spent weeks preparing it, and a beauty it was to behold: scalloped sheets and pillows, stacks of soft-boiled diapers at each end, a patch-quilted cover, my hand-embroidered wedding veil to guard against the insects.

"Nothing worse than bugs!" I must have groaned a thousand times.

They formed a shroud around my baby, a halo over his head. They whirled and danced and dove and tried to bite him on his eyelids, on his ears. They tried to burrow down inside his hair to feed on his pink scalp, but I would watch, and I would squash them. I was a fiercely protective mother from the start. Ask anyone who lived in Paraguay: it was always the bugs that unnerved us. Not the heat that broiled us to a crisp. Not the snakes and scorpions. Not the poverty and lack of proper nutrients and postage stamps. Nothing was worse than the hovering haze, whining and waiting to feed on our flesh.

I set my baby's crib in tiny tins of kerosene to guard against the ants. Now I shudder at the risk I took — what with the spark-throwing fire we kept burning in a pail in the middle of our bedroom on those cold, dank winter nights that followed his glorious birth on that beautiful morning in May. It was clear that the angels protected my baby. Once or twice I found a snake beneath his crib, but it was only a small one, a chilled one. It slunk reluctantly into the bushes when I poked it with a broom. My child slept well. My baby was protected. My son would grow up strong and smart and be a joy to me.

CHAPTER FOUR

Herr Doktor

I WAS COUNSELED left and right by my neighborly matrons that the milk I fabricated for my son was not worth a single bean. He cried too much. He always seemed to be hungry.

Ever since the Days of the Rumor of the Padded Bra, I was a little sensitive about my modest endowment. I knew full well I could not match the bosoms of my older, chubbier friends. Therefore, reluctantly I put my baby's head upon my sweaty shoulder and took him to the doctor for advice.

We called him *Herr Doktor* and stood in awe of him since he was not a Mennonite. As I recall, he was a Lithuanian. He came to us in the wake of an imposter by the tongue-twisting name of Joachim Fertsch. "Doctor" Fertsch had done sheer havoc to our sensibilities. He had been a capricious man, of dangerous demeanor. Rumor had it that he was an Auschwitz henchman on the run — or a vet, perhaps, but certainly no doctor. How he had managed to alight on the unsuspecting Mennonites nobody knew for sure, but he disgraced us from the start. He scandalized the villages, drinking and gambling and stalking holy premises with loaded pistols in his boots until the elders took him by the ears and flung him from our midst.

"A bandit," people who knew him recall.

How could I admit to such a feared authority that I was
cient where it counted most? I thought about that as I
ed through the bush on my way to Number Five. I would
e to think up a ploy to soften the blow of his chastising
gue. I would have to feed him clues to help him guess, to
en my embarrassment and salvage whatever I could of my
manly pride.

There was a bump on Erwin's groin. It seemed to harden
en he cried. It was not big. It came and went under pressure.
nought that it needed attention. And so I said, to get to my
int in a roundabout way:

"I think he has a hernia. That's why he cries. He cries a lot,
err Doktor. He cries and cries and cries. Do you think that's
y he cries?"

"Oh, but then I'll have to operate," said he, with all the
ght of Pontius Pilate.

"Operate?" I cried, aghast.

"Yes. Operate." said Pontius Pilate sharply. "Or what,
iss Wise-owl, do *you* have in mind?" That was the nickname
e had given me when I had been a child, when I had sometimes
itnessed Mama and *Herr Doktor* clash. "Do you perhaps have
better suggestion?"

I was reduced to dust. "Oh, no. Oh, no," I stammered, red
o the rim of my dress. I always turned red when people needled
me about my inconvenient intelligence.

"Well, then . . . !"

Of such words are nightmares made. Why didn't I question — not even once? This man decided on major surgery on the
basis of my inexperienced guess. And there I stood, utterly
cowed, feeling foolish and strangely guilty for doubting his
word, undiapering my baby with trembling hands for him to
take a look and poke and verify what I already knew would be
the outcome. "Why, yes," *Herr Doktor* said, squeezing and
poking and probing away. "That's an iguinal hernia, all right.
I'll have to cut the little fellow. That's for sure."

I remember I asked him, quavering:

"But isn't that terribly dangerous?"

A handful of "nurses" did what the
while Canadian brethren kept searching f
found a willing follower in a youn
chap — straight out of medical school. V
Herr Doktor. He stood many notches abc
diagnostic proclamations were accepted a

I know he saved many a life. I know h
stayed with us for years, and in the end, I h:
his splendid mind from overwork and hea
know if this is true. He was a curious n
haughty in his dealings with the settlers, sha
style. Rumors, based on fears of losing him,
he had only come to train his skills, that one
himself sufficiently, he would leave us agai
plight in the bush.

We said he was knife-happy. We said tha
I want to be fair. No doubt he had genu
Intellectually, he must have been a very lone
have sought his compensation in the extravag
he could take — and nobody any the wiser. H
despot. Girls flocked to him to be trained as hi
I had worked for him as an aide in the colony's
but could not "advance" thanks to a smolderi
him and my mother who, when it came to patie
or two opinions of her own.

I had always feared him secretly, and had
the nurses who were permitted to do more thai
work in the operating room, assisting in the acr
scalpel. Not that that was always fun! Across
gore of an opened belly he would lash out at the
competence, at their stupidity. Despite his gr
despite his fine and virtuous traits, the fact is th
and yelled and terrified and bullied, and he must
and bullied me.

"No, no," he said, briskly. "We just have to watch it a little. It's easy to douse a very young child. Anesthesia, at his age, is a little risky. We'll just have to watch it, that's all . . . "

Whatever else he might have been, this doctor was no fool. I tell myself he must have known the risks he took—he *should* have known! I also tell myself with wrenching guilt of twenty years that *I* should have known, that *I* should have stopped him. Many years later, doctors would ask: "Was that elective surgery?" I never even knew I had a choice. I wrapped my baby, now six weeks, three days of age and—shoes in hand, for it had rained all day, and the street had turned into a muddy morass—slushed along the path down to the hospital entrance to check my baby in for surgery and sign his normalcy away.

Wrapped loosely in gauze, smelling faintly of ether, Erwin lay, tiny and wan, fine tremors all over his body, in a young nurse's sweaty arms. A brief shadow of fear passed over my heart. Was he all right?

"Is he all right?"

"Oh, yes. Oh, yes," said the girl, feeling immensely important. "He arrested on the table. Twice. He almost died, the naughty boy. But *Herr Doktor* quickly revived him . . . "

I had waited all morning, sitting outside on a bench, for the waiting room was full of spitting natives. I looked at the nurse. She was a simple farm girl, not known for her quickness of mind. She had an eye defect as well—her pupils flickered wildly. "*Herr Doktor* knew exactly what to do," she told me now, trying to steady her gaze. "In no time at all he brought him back to life . . . "

I blankly stared at her. What she said had no meaning at all. Why, Erwin lived—that was the only thing I knew. I was so glad to have him back—in much whimpering pain, admittedly, but alive and flushed scarlet and kicking.

As the years wore on, the lore surrounding this life-and-death drama added greatly to *Herr Doktor's* splendid medical repute. "Remember the baby?" people would say. "Why, he jumped his heart with wires and a flashlight battery . . . "

To this day, I do not know what happened. I have been told that the girl with the eye defect overdosed him. Why, she could not see a tree across the street; how could she count small drops of ether from a drop bottle? And can a baby's heart be jumped as if it were a car? That sunny morning—or, for that matter, any other time—our venerable doctor did not bother to explain.

I had no strong premonition. I had never heard of brain cell death. Awed, I looked at my whimpering child, thinking, so small, and already major surgery! Surely so much kicking must connote a lot of spunk and strength? As I held my finger tips to my baby's pounding, racing heart, I did not know that not again for years would he be still, relaxed, at peace, unless in sleep or in total collapse. The horror, for all of us, had begun. But not one word was I told.

I unwrapped him to look.

It seemed a small and innocent enough incision, no more than three inches or so. Translated to a larger body, it might have been impressive. It stretched the length of Erwin's groin. The doctor had lowered one of the testicles and tied it with a hefty stitch to the upper part of his thigh. Every kick would strain the bloody scar and the tiny swollen bluish scrotum. My baby clearly was in agony. I took my scarf from my neck and tied it over his legs to restrain him. This seemed to increase his discomfort, but I had no choice—he was kicking so hard and fast and furiously he was about to rip himself to pieces, poor thing, poor howling, screaming, kicking thing!

I tried to nurse him. He would not suck. He had no strength at all to hold onto my nipple. His lips, his mouth did not close. He never again could be fed from my breast.

He cried and begged and whimpered all night. And the next. And the following night. He could not stop kicking, and, in fact, did not again sleep all through the night for more than a decade. Ten years.

No mother could have been more ignorant than I about the nature of the trauma to his brain. In our villages there must have been a mind or two one might have called "abnormal." There was Hansi, grown now, giggling just a little bit too much. And Gretchen, who perhaps behaved a little odd. There was this one or that one a little peculiar—misfits to be pitied and endured. They were not at all within my own periphery.

Surgery had totally destroyed my son's capacity to nurse, and now I found I could not bottle-feed him adequately, no matter how I tried.

To start, I had no baby nipple.

A mother in the jungle cannot buy a nipple even if she has a bag of gold. Most babies in the villages were nursed, by design or by default, and those who could not be nursed, I had always assumed, must simply die. Would my baby die? I pinched his nostrils shut. I forced him to open his mouth. I tried to spoon in nutritious rice water and milk and mild *yerba mate*. He choked and sputtered, turning purple, and I would have to grab his heels and flip him upside down until he gasped and came to life once more. It was as if I were feeding a sparrow.

Mortified at having a wife as useless as I, Woldi was forced to scour the homesteads: " . . . do you have a nipple hidden somewhere in a sewing box . . . ?" What a shameful thing to have to do!

Persistence did pay off. He somehow hunted down a chewed-up piece of plastic that had belonged to an abandoned Indian child. The thing was old and smelly and brittle, but what a rare and precious find! I guarded it with fervor. It became my most treasured possession. This nipple, to this day, still haunts me in my dreams. The sun is about to dissolve it. It swells and swells and swells. Before my horrified eyes, I see it devoured by ants. A mean and scraggly rooster carries it away. I want to run, as only dreams can make us run, to retrieve it. I will toss and turn and whimper: "Please, baby. Please. Just one more time! Oh, please . . . "

He tried.

He truly did, poor little creature. But his lips, bluish and limp, had no strength at all—he twisted and struggled and exhausted himself on his tremulous task. How could simple sucking be such a draining, heartbreaking chore? We kept a cow close by, milking it as needed to make sure he had fresh milk. I boiled rice and strained it and tried to feed the slimy liquid to my gasping, dying child. I bought *maizena* and mixed it with sugar and struggled against his wild, choking spasms. I squeezed oranges and tried to wet his lips, only to cause watery blisters. Like an Indian, I would chew solid food on his behalf, and put it on his lips and hope and coax and pray. We had, of course, no baby food in Paraguay. My knowledge of raising an infant was nil. I was alone on our homestead, doing solitary battle that first year—a year we came to call, in gallow's humor and apt summary, the Year of Erwin's Nipple.

In the end, a cat snatched the nipple from a tree on which I had stuck it to dry.

On orders from our doctor, all children in the villages had to be vaccinated against small pox, and Erwin's reaction was vile. I had tried to cool him in a trough of water when I saw the cat's mean lurch and felt my heart sink straight into my heels. I could not drop my child and run since he was wet and slippery, and when I could, it was too late. To me, it felt like a sentence of death. I held him with hammering heartbeat. This was the end. His head flopped about. His little arm was pus-infected, swollen more than twice its size. His eyes rolled back in his head. He had a roaring fever. He was covered head to toe with prickly heat. He needed liquid badly, but with the nipple gone, how could he drink? Half-crazed from heat and worry, I rocked him and hugged him, pacing the yard, hoping my presence would somehow convey some ease to my suffering child.

"Oh, my God," cried a neighbor, seeing us thus. "Oh, my God!"

I stared at her dully. Her God? Surely not *my* God who would permit such suffering.

"Where's Woldi?" she asked.

"Woldi sleeps," I told her, tears and venom in my voice. "Try to wake him if you can. I have tried. I can't. He's inside, sleeping like a log."

For weeks and weeks on end, Woldi had worked double time in the sawmill. At that time, he was earning the equivalent of ninety cents per day for fourteen, fifteen hours of work. He was proud of his work and his pay. Compared to the rest of the settlers, we were considered "rich." We always had flour to see us from bake-day to bake-day. Woldi took pride in the things we could buy—ketchup and sardines, even imported potatoes for Christmas. I knew how hard he worked, how much he tried to do, for when he reached for me to hold me close, his hands were rough as iron from the calluses he had acquired in order to give us some measure of ease. And now that Christmas had come, now that three days without work stretched before him, could he not rightfully sleep?

I tried to wake him—in vain.

I sat, shaking with fury and fear, on the edge of his cot, the baby on my knees, trying to make him wake up and look at his son and hear the story of the catnapped nipple and help me think of something—anything!—that would ease Erwin's agony. I pulled his pillow out from under him and threatened to bring a bucket of water—an idle threat, for would I waste a drop of water I had to carry on my aching shoulders the length of Number Eight? Even now, in memory, my adrenaline soars. My spouse slept on and on, and when I grabbed him by the ears, he only turned and mildly shook me off to resume his blissful snore. I sobbed out hateful words and threats and accusations, but he slept on and on as if he were drugged—as indeed he might have been from heat and overwork and lack of proper food.

"Wake up! Wake up!"

No use.

Sometimes, even now, I think that was the first time when I knew, deep down, that my marriage would not last.

Very late in the day, in a festive mood, Woldi rose, restored, ready for the celebration of the birthday of the Lord. By then, Erwin lay silent and limp in his crib. I sobbed: "Look at him! Just look at him, you monster . . . "

"Well, what do you want me to do?" cried Woldi, very hurt. "Just what can I do? Can I fabricate a nipple out of air? I can't. You know that!"

There was raging murder in my heart. I screamed at him like the shrew that the day's utter horror had made me. I shouted that he did not care. I said he was a boy—a ninny!—he did not know how to grow up. I sobbed that he had responsibilities. I screamed that I hated him—I pulled that from deep, deep recesses within me. I could not help saying the things that I said, all kinds of horrid accusations, twisted, unacknowledged things that now came tumbling out. I said horrible things, over and over. Woldi watched me silently as if I had lost every shred of sanity, as indeed I must have on that day. Without a further word, he went calmly to saddle his horse. I heard him ride away, and I stood in the dark, alone, despairing, wishing that I and my baby would die.

I was too ashamed to send someone to find him. An absent husband at Christmas could simply not be explained. I felt despair beyond all words. I was resigned to Erwin's death. It was, I thought dully, just a matter of hours, at best or at worst. I was so drained and tired, in the end, that I no longer cared.

Famished and sweaty and covered with dust, but in a gay conqueror's spirit, Woldi returned in due time with a set of nipples sticking out of his pocket—still cellophane-wrapped, believe it or not! What are diamonds? What are rubies? What are roses? Give me brand new baby nipples any day! I put my arms around my husband's neck and cried and cried and cried.

By and by, I heard the rest.

He had ridden to Rosario, a trip that took all night. Rosario was the closest native town that had a merchant sage enough to store such an unlikely item. But when my love arrived in Rosario, he found out that it was Christmas in Rosario, too—every single store was closed, and Woldi being Woldi thought it unseemly to knock on a door. Patiently, he therefore camped himself by a tree to outwait the holiday silence. In due time, he found what he had come to buy. Thereupon, his problem neatly solved, he once again outwaited the worst of the heat by visiting a native friend to drink some rounds of *mate,* and then my love trod slowly home.

With the flair of a knight having conquered a kingdom, here he was now, his purchase in proud, dirty hands, smiles all over his good, friendly face, gently scolding me for being, under stress, just a little bit too loony—no? Take now—could I calm down a little? Could I stop shaking and carrying on? Why, the baby still lived—wasn't that so? Brave little fellow? Sturdy, feisty little boy?

Yes, Erwin lived. I don't know how.

That Christmas, at six months of age, he weighed less than when he was born.

CHAPTER FIVE

Farewell to the Jungle

HE COULD NOT SIT, not even with pillow support. He drooled. His eyes would strain to focus in the morning; as the day wore on, they rolled behind grey lids. There was no way he could hold up his head. He kicked and screamed and choked and cried. I kept him in a wooden oblong basin that I carried everywhere—to the well at the end of the village, into the shade of a tree as I hung his diapers to dry in the blistering sun, into the fields to dig for *manioc,* even to the outhouse—just to be sure, what with his coughing and gasping and wheezing!

When he slept, I tried to sleep. When he woke to yet another stretch of torment, I would walk him back and forth. My shoulder blades flamed. My head spun like a top. I had no air; I could not eat; I cried at the slightest cross word from my husband. In the end, I had so exhausted myself in body and soul that there were times when I would run away from this struggle without end, far enough into the fields for just a few minutes of silence. There I would slouch on some tree stump, fists to my ears, thinking my mind must explode.

Once I dragged my baby's crib, tin cans of kerosene and all, across the yard to the abandoned shack where *Mutter* used to live before she left for Canada. We did not use the building any longer, for it was crumbling and sagging and spider-infested, but it had a door that could be closed and windows to be bolted. I sobbed that we should leave him there, that nothing would happen, that we must let him cry—for just one night of sleep, just a few hours of rest and reprieve!

Of course I didn't sleep. I could still hear his shrieks. He shrieked as if someone had cruelly impaled him. After an hour, I dragged myself back, a dutiful mother. I lifted him out of his crib. I held him close in the darkness. A curious sensation swept over my body—a crawling, biting, pinching sensation. Of late, my body, my mind flashed unreliable signals. I felt chills in the heat of high noon. I woke drenched in sweat in the chill of early morning. Clearly, my nerves were in spasms again. Surely, this itching would cease just as soon as I could manage to stop shaking. I fumbled for a match. There was a cord that hung from a window. The night air had moved it, had pushed it onto the edge of the crib. In the brief flash of flame I saw that it was black, it all but coiled with insects—a hanging bridge, thick with ants! I ran back into the house and doused us both with fistfuls of a powerful insecticide we kept at hand to mix into the dough of mud, manure, and *manioc* with which we laid our indoor floors. For two days afterwards, I wiped dead ants out of my baby's nose and ears.

Early in January, at the height of the summer, the mail brought us a heavy stack of papers that told us we could leave for Canada. Permission, we learned, lay stapled and filed in Niagara Falls. A sponsor had offered a job. *Mutter* was weepingly urging us on in a long, laborious letter. We wouldn't be so foolish as to stay when a few weeks in Canada could earn us more than decades had thus far? Albert had figured that out on a clean piece of paper. She had underlined his argument for us to take to heart.

Albert ruled family matters by tacit agreement, having been a store clerk once, a coveted position. So Albert had decreed that we must go? Would Woldi take that meekly? I so hungered to be able to see strength and independence in my man. I so wanted him to say: ". . . yes, we will go . . . " or " . . . no, we will stay," and know those words contained an independent judgment. I said, to prod him: "Well, what do you say? Should we go, or should we stay?"

"Of course, we'll go," said Woldi. "Since Albert has gone to the trouble."

"And what about our dreams and hopes?"

I said that to have the last word. For in my heart I was no longer sure. I looked at my whimpering child. The heat, that day, had dazed me. I had not eaten anything since early morning; my rebellious stomach muscles heaved and churned at the thought of any food. I said weakly, forsaking all housewifely duties: "I cannot cook tonight. I think I better lie down for a while . . . "

"That's all right," said Woldi. "I caught some fish in the mudhole. I'll fry them. Do you want to eat some, too . . . ?" He held the wiggling creatures in his wet *maleta,* a double pouch of burlap cloth slung for convenience and expediency across his horse's back. I leaned my head against a post, feeling drops of perspiration trickle down my spine. I watched him as he dumped the fish into a handy bucket. He started scaling them, still live. The water turned slimy. I knew those fish were full of worms — all living creatures harbored worms in Paraguay, including little babies. Woldi whistled with contentment. I could hear the pig lard sizzle sharply as he went about his task. I could see the pieces, still contracting, in the greasy frying pan. All the trees around me reeled. It occurred to me, in a panic beyond words, that I might be pregnant again. The thought filled me with absolute horror.

Woldi washed his hands forevermore of his hated sawmill job and announced the length of Number Eight that Albert had instructed us to take the next ship down the river. Albert had secured an ample loan with easy terms and extended repayments. Albert drove a car in Canada. Albert would wait for us at the Toronto International Airport.

I heard all that from neighbors who arrived to wish us luck.

I felt my way into the hut and sat down with shaky knees to

write to brother Albert: "Yes, we will come." Sensing my desperate mood, Woldi put his arms around me, saying gently: "Well, why bother? They don't need a letter. Albert *knows* we'll come . . . "

By the time our visas were ready, Erwin had strenghtened enough to hold up his head. If I supported his back, he could sit in my lap in some fashion.

We sold what little we had: my hand-embroidered sheets and pillows, six curtains in good shape, four matching knives and forks and spoons, Woldi's sturdy saddle, two rakes, three hoes, our drinking water *cantaro*. We sold our few cattle and horses.

We could not sell our land — there were no takers any longer. The jungle had fought the intruders; the jungle had won. I knew that. I knew just how fully the jungle had won. It would enter our bedroom, our kitchen in a wave of tangled lava and engulf fourteen years of backbreaking work. In less than two years, not a trace would be left of the fact that once we had lived here, that here we had loved and suffered and fought. How simple it was, and how vast.

Down the river we went to the city, about to board a plane. To me, a plane was part of fairyland, a silvery speck in the sky, held up in the clouds by what means I could not fathom, and cannot, really, to this day. It's still worldly magic — no doubt about that. Now a plane would fly us out of Paraguay into a land and future I could not, for the life of me, imagine.

I remember I seatbelted Erwin, bolting for the lavatory hastily. I spent most of my time there for the rest of the turbulent flight that took more than three days, with stops in San Paolo, Brazil, and Caracas, Venezuela. I remember being airborne and awash in one great wave of nausea. I was pregnant all right — of that there was no doubt. In between gulps for air I thought dizzily: "Can it really be true we have left the jungle for good?" A weight had dropped from me. Even as my vision blurred and my churning insides kept me on my knees above the chlorine-scrubbed commode, I knew that, for once, my clan had been right. I would have an easier life in Canada — if only I could keep myself demure.

Whenever I could, I emerged, water in the marrow of my knees but in my heart enough curiosity to steal last looks out of a tiny window: the sweltering jungle below me, engulfed in veils of smoke as if it were emerging from a dying fire — a swaying green carpet, soft and deceptive, gentle and good when viewed from such heights. Would I miss it — the only life that I had ever really known? The cascades of sun rays that killed like honed swords? The pretty butterflies churning out their gobs of maggots? The whirring voices diving for all skin, the slinking long armies of ants, the complicated, brutal battle for existence? Would I miss it even once?

It hurt my pride to have to say it, but I knew that I would not.

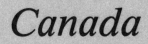

Canada

CHAPTER SIX

Hello to Ice and Snow

WE STAGGERED, PALE, through Canadian customs in Toronto on May 10th of 1960.

We thought that we were rich—after having paid the various governmental bribes for getting out of Paraguay, we still owned precisely $100! It was more money in one heap than we had ever seen. I kept it in an envelope securely rubber-banded to my wrist.

My letter must have gone astray. There was no one to meet us.

We took a cab, not knowing how to telephone. The hour-long ride to our destination, the lovely city of St. Catharines, cost $31. Our first month's rent for a small, dark apartment took another $45. That still left $24—enough for two weeks' worth of groceries.

Not bad. Not one iota different from other immigrants who made a start with less than we.

A loan advanced to us from a Mennonite bank to pay for our airline tickets amounted to more than $400, and that was a bargain, as well I should know—what with that blind extra passenger deep down within me! We would speedily have to repay it, of course. Our future lay clouded before us, but we had stepped into a dizzy world: water spigots that never emptied, highways criss-crossing the length and width of Canada, milk delivered to the door and not a cow in sight, polka-dotted table napkins, weeks of grace before a bill fell due, geometric flower beds with not a weed between them, noisy things that cut and vacuumed lawns. No longer did I have to cart my household water, or sweep my earthen floors with reedy, shedding brooms. The broom I used in Canada had bristles as soft as a toothbrush, and just as straight and clean. I had never seen a lovelier household item.

A telephone call summoned them all: *Mutter* on a cloud of strident elation now that, at last, she could count heads and not miss one; Victor and Kate, who lived and worked in Virgil; Albert and Tina; assorted friends and former neighbors. The men squeezed my hand, but then ignored me pointedly, laying claim to my husband at once: " . . . let's go look at Albert's car." I could hear their laughter from the kitchen. The women filled my cup with steaming, pitch-black coffee while I listened to the drift of Mennonite life amid the lure of worldly Canada:

" . . . do you remember Susie from village Number Five? Well, can you imagine . . . "

I could, and I did. Pants without creases, shirts without starch — that's what Canada had wrought of Susie, formerly so prim and meek. Piped music to her basement. A typing class behind her in-laws' backs. Store-bought cakes. Visiting with English neighbors. It could all but break a mother's heart.

I remembered Susie well. She and I grew up together. When she left for Canada, I had missed her as a happy, kindred soul. I had looked forward to visiting her, but now I found out that I had better not — poor Susie had slipped, and the temptations of the world had all but done her in:

" . . . for breakfast she eats cottage cheese . . . "

" . . . and she makes her husband walk the dogs . . . "

Mutter sat, starched to the tips of her fingers, filled to the brim with righteous wrath. Kate echoed disapproval. Tina cast snapping glances in my direction, meant to speak louder than words. When Mennonites gossip, even the dogs stop wagging their tails.

"... and her towels are embroidered 'His' and 'Hers' ... "

" ... so what of that?" I said. I, too, had never heard of such a thing, but what a fancy notion! "Before you know it, I might do that, too ... "

Tina blushed at such immodesty. Kate exploded into gales of laughter to take the edge off my remark. *Mutter* stabbed at a piece of cold chicken to show her angry disapproval. But then I could see she forgave me, after pondering it duly, for the sake of harmony. Why, this was life at its best: a kitchen filled with relatives, all mulling about, all eating and talking, passing judgment on poor Susie and her ways. What harm in merry judgmental chit-chat? If you belonged, you could not find a warmer group, but pity the one who was different.

I sat among them, my differences all over me like jaundice. I felt goaded by a mad, mad longing with no name. This was a world not large enough to hold me. I knew it. Within hours of our arrival, I knew that with finality. I sat there and sipped bitter coffee and knew that I did not belong. Clannish and self-contained, that's what they were, feeling a profound and bitter hatred for all that was not of their world, be it words or things or deeds. Even here in Canada they would live a carbon-copy life, but most assuredly without me — no, no, and triple no. I would not buy those identical Tupperware dishes! I would not sew and stuff those same old boring quilts!

There is no way to say it gently — ours was a narrow world. We watched each other jealously and stealthily for the tiniest of transgressions. We tattled. We told on each other, policing each other's deportment. Here I was, a stepchild in a close-knit family, married and hence without leeway, and as early as tomorrow an elder would knock on my door. The very thought filled me with rancor. I sat among them, empty and exhausted, dizzy from the unaccustomed taxi ride. I had forgotten what it felt like to live within this unrelenting scrutiny, in a kind of cloying, clawing, wet proximity that left no room to breathe. Hadn't I known it before—all the underhanded bickering, the backbiting, the double-talk, all the secrets and connivances, the petty, small comparisons such as the number, size, and mix of pickle jars, the furtive poking into dark and shameful corners, the finding of faults in all people of lesser righteousness than we?

" . . . do you remember so-and-so from village Number Five . . . ?"

Ask anyone who knows our slate of soul—few are the vices a Mennonite harbors. We do not sleep into a weekday morning, or break a promise we have made, or pardon the unworthy. We never work on a Sunday, or neglect to say grace before every meal, or take our Saviour's name in vain. A Mennonite of the authentic cloth will not lie, cheat, steal, dance, or gamble. He covets not his neighbor's wife nor ass. He supports his congregation's tithe and his country's income tax. He won't hum a song having sprung from a Beatle, or pick up a hitchhiking hoodlum, or get a divorce. He will never take ashtrays or soap from the Holiday Inn. He will not trade punches or bloody an enemy's nose, throw dishes in anger, idle away a vacation, or entertain a lusty thought. But he will gossip with a vengeance. It is vicious. It is constant. And it hurts.

I knew within minutes of having landed there in Tina's immaculate kitchen that Erwin would make me a target—that I would be bloodied by gossip but good.

" . . . a fussy eater, huh?" said *Mutter,* warming up, and Tina helped her quickly: " . . . yes, look at those poor legs . . . "

Kate, who absorbed all her opinions from her in-laws, echoed merry reinforcement: " . . . yes, look at his arms *and* his legs . . . "

"Poor, poor thing . . . " said *Mutter,* breathing hard.

"I wonder why . . . ?" speculated Tina.

"Are you feeding him right . . . ?" Kate wanted to know.

"We'll have to show you how to feed him," offered *Mutter.*

She held Erwin in her lap and covered him with many compensating kisses. Tina and Kate passed meaningful glances between them. Tina rolled her eyes beseechingly to let me know as sister to sister that nothing had changed—sooner or later *Mutter* would meddle, I could count on that. From the corner of her eyes she would scrutinize my skills and draw expedient conclusions about my worth and let the neighbors know. Kate's eyes were opened wide in a kind of elevated disbelief—why, barely had I arrived, and already a war? Kate had always treated me with awe and admiration—the only one in my acquired family to do so from the bottom of her simple, ample heart. Kate giggled. I swallowed. *Mutter*, suspicious, wanted to know: "What's wrong? What's wrong? Is anything wrong?"

"Nothing."

"You're upset."

"I'm not upset."

"I can see you're upset. Why are you upset?"

"I'm not. I'm just tired."

"Tell me what's wrong. Is anything wrong?"

"Nothing."

Everything. Everything was wrong as anything could be. I was being decimated systematically—that's all I could feel, a kind of slow diminishment coming from these chatty gossips with whom I had nothing in common, for whom I could not feel a closeness, no matter how I tried. It is impossible to struggle against gravity. I knew within hours of having come to Canada that it would take much patience, guile, and skill to navigate my questing soul within this chitchat and this drivel. From the depth of my soul I would have to marshall a generous spirit of truce, and I was not sure that I could.

I fled to join the men outside, but Woldi turned on me as well: " . . . do you always have to be two steps behind me . . . ?" making it clear I was shaming him greatly by mingling brash and brazen with the men. I could see that Woldi envied Albert, and surely with good cause, for a beauty it was, Albert's car, a '56

Dodge, gleaming with expensive wax, rubbed down and patted dry. My envious husband stood enthralled. My love climbed into and out of the seats, peering under the hood, rapping filters and hoses with appreciative knuckles: " . . . oh my oh my oh my . . . " I could not resist pointing out: " . . . at least I won't have to feed it sugar cane . . . " and Woldi whispered fervently: " . . . go on up! Go on up! Join the women . . . "

So I climbed the stairs again and sat amid the ladies, silently.

Our basement bedroom had no windows. Jungle nights are lit and warm and live and full of tiny voices, and through the thickets gleam the stars. There were no stars at all in Canada. There was a single sound: a truck roared by, shaking our only piece of furniture, a rusty bed frame that Albert had prudently bought and hauled into our empty apartment from a Salvation Army store.

CHAPTER SEVEN

Growth?

IN PARAGUAY, WE CLAPPED our hands to warn the dogs when visiting. Not so in Canada—in Canada, one simply put a finger to a button on the wall next to each door! Everything seemed strange and elegant. I remember the awe I felt at seeing traffic lights change, the glittering telephone poles flying by as we drove along the Queen Elizabeth on Sunday afternoons to visit long-time friends. With keen ear, I listened to the car horns crowing louder than roosters did at their lusty best. Every time our "fridge" jumped, prodded by the current, so did I.

And for the never-ending wonders of a stacked super-market store! Frozen chicken legs, already plucked and cleaned. Sliced bread. Canned soups. Candies sorted, stacked by kind and color. Pickled fish and chocolate milk. Sugar either cubed in boxes or in cartons with a spout. Dried potatoes I could store forever in my cupboard in anticipation of a rainy day. Paper towels, soft and luxurious. I would buy them just to feast on lavish looks. And the glory of a layered brick of ice cream! "Tutti frutti . . . " I would say, blushing crimson, feeling wicked to the core. What a salacious name for ice cream!

Every shopping trip was an adventure. Doors flew open at my touch, closed behind me magically. I entertained a fantasy that the store kept scores of gremlins hidden somewhere, pulling invisible strings for my sole, delighted convenience, opening glass doors as if for a queen. At times I would tease the helpful little critters, but they were much smarter than I.

Erwin seemed to strenghten by the day, although *Mutter* said unkindly to a neighbor, who then passed the remark to me, that he was as floppy as an octopus. At night, he still slept fitfully, and so did I, trying to keep him from waking the landlord. But I did not have to worry: no snakes in Canada to curl around his neck, no dog in need of a warm spot, no chicken to hop on his pillow to find a snug place for an egg.

"Just wait and see," I told Tina proudly, dizzy with hope. "He's older than your Walter. He's bound to overtake him yet." I was convinced that this was so, although compared to Tina's little son, my child was clearly at a woeful disadvantage. Tina lived above us on the second floor, while we humbly occupied the lowest level, with the landlord, Mr. Peters, in between. Mr. Peters was the one who supplied our livelihood. Woldi and Albert worked for him, wrecking old houses for the incredible sum of $8.00 per day. Mr. Peters was a watered-down Canadian of Mennonite descent.

Tina and I became wary friends. She introduced me to the miracles of vitamins and baby food, and I was sure that Erwin's progress was just a matter of time and sufficient boxes and glass jars of *Gerber's*.

"He's changing for the better by the day," I told Tina.

"Is that so?" said Tina, doubtfully.

I was convinced of it.

I bathed him with fragrant baby soap and tucked in his toes just so, and I could see the change: on good days he would actually coo. With a fleeting smile, he would try to look at me and seem to want to hold my glance. Then I was happy. Then I was breathless with joy. Soon he attempted to crawl. He seemed to drag his left side, which made me laugh, since I attributed this funny crawl to baby ingenuity. Friends had lent us a playpen so that I could keep him in my kitchen as I prepared his food on a stove that gleamed with the efforts of my scouring. What ease of living—just standing there, turning a faucet, pushing a button or two! Gone were the days of chopping wood and drawing murky water from a half-forgotten village well and slapping at ants and mosquitos.

And there came the wondrous day when my baby clutched onto the bars with spindly fingers and hauled himself up to a standing position. I started to cry in sheer shaking relief.

"He stood by himself," I told Woldi.

"You made that up," said Woldi, to be on the safe side.

"I did not!" I insisted, resenting his needling. Well, yes, he did collapse right afterwards and chipped a brand new tooth. Now he refused to repeat the performance. But I knew what I knew, and I told what I knew. And one day, with Tina for a witness, Erwin grabbed hold of his training pants for additional balance and with a wobble and a howl ran clear across the room.

He ran!

He did not walk, he galloped. On quivering legs, he staggered a distance of more than twelve feet. I sat, bloated like a toad by now with my second pregnancy, tears of gladness in my throat. Thank God he ran like any other child! Perhaps, with a proper mix of patience, luck and wisdom, I could manage after all. For soon, there would be two to teach—two little ones when one had seemed so overwhelming.

Here was the truth, a shameful thing: I did not want another baby. Not so soon. Not while Erwin was still such a difficult struggle, howling and shrieking through many a night. Not while an impatient landlord knocked on the floor with a broom and threatened to evict us unless we kept the baby quiet. Not while we still lived like moles in a dark hole, in a shabby, three-room apartment that never saw a ray of sun.

And on a deeper, less acknowledged level: Not with Woldi clearly ill-at-ease with my second pregnancy.

It seemed to me that Woldi dreaded depths of feelings, that his inner needs were plain and simple, and my needs were difficult and vast. I was starved for sympathy, hungry for attention, mad for compassionate love. I so wanted Woldi's arms around me when I was so afraid. I wanted him to tell me pretty things — I wanted him to say in beautiful, romantic words that in his eyes, though huge and clumsy like an elephant by now, I still had grace and beauty and worth. I wanted him to say he loved me. He never did. Not once.

I never went anywhere now, for fear of being seen and judged. I waited for the darkness to take my solitary walks around the block, pushing Erwin in a squeaky buggy. Once I asked Woldi to accompany me to a store to buy a quart of milk, and while he went quite willingly, he told me by the door: "Wait here."

I felt it for weeks, like a slap in my face.

It happened that, a few days later, I ran into a very pregnant girl, older than I, and certainly uglier. She wore a cheap pink organdy blouse and a skirt that was sloppily tied to her back, but her husband's hands went gently through her hair, and he bent toward her lovingly and made her smile with joy. I saw it very clearly — that special loving touch of intimacy I had studied furtively, watching handsome actors on Kate's scratched TV.

I walked on, blinded by what I had seen.

A few blocks down the street, in front of a department store, I saw myself full length in a mirror, and what I saw I did not like at all. I paused to force myself to take full stock: hair in need of a cut, mouth too large, eyebrows too heavy, skirt too long, shoes too scuffed, stomach sticking out like a balloon.

What a mess!

In my purse I had a little money of my own — cashed in the previous day from the "Canadian baby bonus" the government sent on the 20th of each month. I had meant to save it for a Sunday suit for Erwin, to spruce him up a bit. But as I took my eyes from the alien, unattractive creature in the mirror, the Devil made them fall upon the shelves of a cosmetic stand.

I bought a coral lipstick. A tube of mascara. A bottle of lotion named *Passion's Delight*. A jar of cold cream a movie star was advertising on a poster. And when I counted the pennies still left, I swallowed hard and bought a bottle of fiery red finger nail polish.

CHAPTER EIGHT

The Quarrel

I HAVE ARRIVED AT A POINT I dread so much that I almost did not write this book: I must confront my destructive encounter with *Mutter*. I must speak for us both, for she is now in her grave, our hurt to this day unresolved. She was right. But so was I. We should not have been afflicted with each other. Only through the vast malevolence embedded in banality could it have happened that she and I, irreconcilable and different, would find ourselves set jaw to jaw, and who lost out? A little boy.

She was a simple woman, with God on her side and Jesus on her chatty tongue. I was embroiled deeply in a furtive ferment all my own. The conflict was there from the start, and it started so silly: a gnat's bite, no more.

An elder, a nitwit, mistakenly inflated my age by a decade the day he pulled out of his pocket a folded piece of paper to announce from the pulpit that I would wed her son. Since an elder, in *Mutter's* simple world, was incapable of error, I stood implicated, inferentially, for having snared a husband with a lie. No matter what I said, no matter what evidence I marshalled on behalf of my relative youth, she knew what she knew, and she would let me know she knew: " . . . at *your* age . . . " she would say, and let me know that she had not forgotten. I would correct her: "*Mutter,* I am only twenty-four . . . " and she would sigh to hint she could not be deceived.

A small matter, to be sure. But in those years, I craved acceptance and accord within the framework of the rules that I knew. At first, I liked her well enough and did my share and more to please and smooth and placate. But her fuzzy gullibility proved to be a constant irritant. And her unrelenting need to talk sucked every shred of patience out of me. I saw in her incessant chatter, her gabbiness and gushiness, the narrow limitations of her soul, and for those limitations I rebuffed her.

In church she sat docile, a woman quiet and modest to the eye, tears welling copiously, pondering her lot: three boys and a girl whom she had raised in hardships untold and nowhere recorded, now married to strangers, with lives of their own. She could not grasp that. She could not reconcile herself to being on the sidelines. She was oblivious to anything except her own relentless need — to negate that vast fear that her children now pushed her aside, that nobody needed her, nobody wanted her, nobody cared for a jolly Sunday reunion, no one felt sympathy for her who knew no rest nor rectitude until we all packed up to roar along the Queen Elizabeth to yet another *Kaffeeklatsch,* preferably at Victor's place since Victor had the largest living room and Kate baked the best *Zwieback.*

In my growing need for solitude as I grew large with child, I dreaded the noisy ordeals, and I dodged them whenever I could. A bottomless pit, that's what it was, her need to have us flock together, impossible to satisfy! Come Saturday, she would commence her litany at breakfast time: "Let me do the dishes . . . hurry up . . . let's not dally . . . " In a cloying kind of servitude she would plot and scheme and push and bargain to that end:

" . . . if I hang the laundry, would you meanwhile . . . "

" . . . while I take the baby round the block, would you pack . . . "

" . . . if we leave right now, I might trade you . . . "

Against her unremitting bribery, I would resolutely set my teeth. I did not want to go. And my grim determination not to go fully matched her chatty, gay determination that I would. Week after week, we battled with each other—at first in jest and then, as weeks wore on, in growing bitter anger. She sat on my embroidered cushions, snapping and unsnapping her purse, staring at the door accusingly. Here she was, a martyr, knitting away at a sweater for Erwin, with her Sunday almost gone and her very fingers numbed, and did I give a hoot? Another three hours, and Albert would whisk her away, back to the Vineland Retirement Home where she, in old age, must work as an aide—since nobody—nobody—cared.

"You want to work, *Mutter*. You know that is your choice."

"Ha! Do I have a choice? Who wants me? An old and useless woman."

With an effort: "You know you are welcome to come and live with us."

"What would I do here? I'd just sit here, with nothing to do, nowhere to go. Take today, for instance . . . "

Itching, irking little needlepricks, I told myself in simmering rebellion, each one designed to draw a drop of blood. Others might suffer them for the sake of the Holy Commandments—not I! Worn out by nights without sleep, I did not suffer her calmly. My emotions reeled in her presence. I did not see her loneliness, her need to retain for herself a semblance of feeling important. All I knew with a vexation beyond words was this: here I was, tired and ugly and fat, in a dark, dank basement apartment, on my hands a very sick baby and an incessantly chattering fool.

" . . . if you would only hurry . . . "

Hours ago, she had bundled up her slippers, and still no progress anywhere. She pulled apart my window curtains, peering out with deep, deep sighs. By her watch she could tell how her afternoon trickled away—it was almost too late now for coffee. And Kate had baked a chocolate cake. Four layers high and

iced with yellow sugar. Kate never skipped her Sunday baking.
" . . . whereas you . . . "

"I am sorry."

I was deficient in all ways—notably in hospitality.

"You hardly bake at all. Why don't you bake something next weekend? We could meet at your place for a change . . . "

"I don't have enough chairs. And I don't like to bake, *Mutter*. You know that."

"Yes. You buy ready-made cakes from the grocery store."

I was a spendthrift, too. I bought bread already sliced, no matter that it cost an extra dime. I did not can dills and tomatoes, never mind that the seasons were here. I shopped at the Dominion Store, wasting extra time and mileage going south while Kate and Tina shopped more prudently at the A&P where bargains were plenty and where they had an opportunity to scrutinize the shopping carts of former Paraguayan neighbors.

Pause.

"Have you asked me yet about my day?"

"What?"

"Ask me how my day was."

"How *was* your day, *Mutter*?"

"Which day?"

"Whaaat?"

"Today or yesterday?"

"Take your pick." Icily.

"No, *you* tell *me*."

With a deep, suffering sigh on my part: "All right. Tell me about yesterday."

Sprightly: "Oh, *yesterday!* My, what a day was yesterday! Poor Tante Unruhsche called . . . " Did I remember Tante Unruhsche? She was afraid to touch her daughter's dishes. Yes, that was life, especially in Canada. The old were pushed to the side, the young did the dishes their way. " . . . and Gredel's husband wants to buy a car. Tante Unruhsche likes yellow, not that her opinions count . . . "

She had a high, ingratiating voice. When she finished a round, she would boomerang back to fill in details she had previously missed. Gredel took on worldly ways. Gredel did no longer roll her husband's socks—she pinned them. She pinned them with a special pin that she had bought at Sears on Monday. Or was it Tuesday? It could have been Tuesday—she, *Mutter,* was not sure. Old age did that to you. You were no longer sure of anything, not even the love of your very own children. Either way—a dozen for ninety-nine cents. Couldn't I see it all coming? One thing would lead to the next. Car pool with Canadians. Telephone receivers off the hook. Did poor Tante Unruhsche deserve to be pushed aside, to be treated like that? Just like that? Did anyone? But that was life in Canada. The old no longer counted.

"Hmmm . . . "

"Not that I am surprised." Long ago, she stopped being surprised. That was one thing you learned in Canada. Poor Tante Unruhsche. Her eyesight was failing already. So was her hearing. And soon she would be dead. Then Gredel would be sorry.

" . . . say, that reminds me! Could we take a little ride to Victor's house . . . ?"

I sat, my head throbbing like a boil, feeling cold with dislike and despair. I looked at her. She looked at me, sheepishly, tears welling in her eyes. " . . . if we leave right now . . . "

"I'm not going."

Red blotches had formed on her neck. Another perfect Sunday wasted for no discernible reason. Her agony filled my apartment, filled absolutely everything—a sort of leaden grey despotic need that clutched onto my soul. " . . . it isn't too late. If we get up and hurry . . . " Was I without pity, seeing her sitting there, swallowing tear after tear after tear? Didn't she always accommodate me, hadn't she done me a favor when I vetoed Sears the other day, forsaking the sale she had counted on, where she could have ridden up and down the elevators, her eyes on the Blue Light, watching for on-the-spot bargains? Hadn't she, instead, stayed home with me and helped me fold my sheets?

"I told you I don't want to go." Lack of sleep was shrieking within me. "*Mutter,* I'm not well . . . "

"What's the matter? What's the matter? Are you upset? Did I upset you? What did I do? Say something, will you? Why don't you ever talk to me . . . ?" Silence in and of itself offended her. " . . . don't just sit there silently . . . "

"I *am* talking to you, *Mutter.*"

She gazed at me, puzzled and perplexed, twisting her hands in her lap, clasping and unclasping fingers. Was this a friendly invitation to explain to me why I must go, or a caustic barb meant to silence her obliquely? In a trembling voice, she said: " . . . you make fun of me. I know I am in the way. Does anyone care about me . . . ?"

"Your children do," I know I should have said.

Yes, I rationed my concessions. I could have told her that I cared. But it would not have been enough to tell her: " . . . I care, *Mutter.* Truly I do." I could have managed telling her that. For I did care, I wanted to please. But no. I would then have to hug her, and I would have to hand us both a tissue handy in the cross-stitched apron she had given me. Together we would sit, reassuring each other: Yes, life must go on. Despite three previous wasted Sundays where none of her sons had appeared. Not Albert. Not Victor. Not Woldi. Despondent, she had tried to call, but Tina had outfoxed her. Tina, she knew, had taken the phone off the hook, and she, an old and useless woman, was left all alone, pacing the lawn of the Vineland Retirement Home, with all of her Sunday before her and nothing to do, not even an up-to-date snapshot to look at. Did anybody think of her and come and take her for a ride? Oh, no.

"I do not *want* to go," I cried shrilly, about to snap an invisible coil. "Not today!" Not today. Not next week. Not for the duration of my pregnancy. I did not enjoy being stared at, being whispered at behind my back, now that Walterle was toilet-trained and not a shred of evidence that Erwin progressed there. I didn't want to spend another afternoon wasting energies on disputes as to what recipes to use for *Peppernuts*.

"But I . . . "

She took her coat and mine from hangers. She put them on a chair. She went for ambush, desperately:

"You shouldn't always hide behind your . . . well, you know . . . "

I said with great difficulty: "Yes, I'm pregnant. That's why I do not want to go. And since you brought it up, I want to ask you a favor. Would you come and care for Erwin when I'm . . . when I'm gone? It would really mean a lot to me."

"But you . . . "

I knew. It was the worst of all possible times to have asked for that kind of a favor. I picked my baby from the floor and put him, writhing, in his pen, my vision blurring from the effort. He still did not know how to play, but he had grown a little calmer, and surely a father's mother should not mind? "I really worry about Erwin being safe and taken care of . . . "

"If I'm free," she said, promptly and sweetly. "But right now I know already that I won't be free. I'll have to work. You know that I have to. I have to make a living in my old age . . . "

"You always claim you are no longer needed. I'll need you for my baby to be born."

A silence lay between us like a morass. To break it, she said sprightly: "You know what gets me? What really gets me? You won't do me a favor. Not ever. Not once! But if I can do you a favor . . . "

I felt as if she had thrown me a hook, and now she was pulling it, closer and closer. I was the fish at the end, smarting at the mouth.

"*Mutter,*" I said, mustering every ounce of calm. "I don't have anyone else. And I really can't ride with you every Sunday to Victor and Kate's. I get horribly carsick; I have to throw up. I really need you, *Mutter*. There's no room for Erwin's crib in Tina's tiny bedroom. I've already asked her—she said no. And even though Kate offered . . . " I did not want to think of Kate, sitting on her threadbare carpet, watching *I Love Lucy*, mesmerized. "Kate is not reliable." Kate would lather soap in

Erwin's eyes and feed him mashed potatoes with big lumps. Canada had not brought order and predictability into Kate's perpetual cheerful chaos. " . . . you know how careless Kate can be . . . "

"Yes," agreed *Mutter,* fully in the know. "In her household you can't find a place to put your feet, let me tell you that. Kate is very sloppy. But still, she bakes a gorgeous cake. I know she baked one for today, and now she wonders why we aren't com . . . "

I threw the napkin on the table, violently. My pulse raced. Anger and frustration came in gushes of great heat.

"Why, what's the matter? Where are you going?"

"To the bathroom, *Mutter* . . . "

"Oh, only to the bathroom . . . " And she, so help me, tip-toed after me. "What are you doing inside?" she shouted through the door. "Are you getting yourself finally ready?"

"I am going for a walk!" I shouted back. I threw the door wide open. I put a little stand-up mirror on the table, and in front of that mirror I seated myself. "Yes, I am getting ready to go out. Alone!"

"What are you doing?" cried *Mutter,* aghast.

"This," I said viciously, "is lipstick. Eye shadow. Rouge. Finger nail polish. Vanishing cream." I put it all down on the table. Her eyes turned steely with anguish and shock. I was drunk with my roaring defiance. "I am putting make-up on my face. I am powdering my nose. I am painting my finger nails red. And if I can manage to bend far enough, I might paint my toenails in the bargain . . . "

"What will Woldi say?" she cried, gurgling.

"Ha! What can he say?"

Her face was purple now, streaked. It gave me great pleasure to see that. All day long, she had nag-nag-nagged me half to death, and it was time for me—for me!—to show I would do as I pleased.

"You wouldn't. . . !" she cried, trembling.

"Just watch me!"

I could have predicted the outcome. She was a very simple

soul — she meant no harm to any reasonable creature. But I was now The Enemy. She had tried as best she could to welcome me into her arms despite my many hooks and prickles. And had I lived a humble, straight-laced life, I'm sure she would have seen to it that not a bit of harm would come my way. But right was right, and wrong was wrong, and what I was about to do was wrong, and so she cried, filled with a dark and bitter malice:

"Some people smear their lips with goo so that not even husbands want to kiss them . . . "

What happened now came gushing. Neither one of us had known that it was there. I said sharply: "Be quiet! My husband loves me."

"That's what *you* think," she said, slowly and maliciously. "Nobody loves you. You hear me? Nobody. Nobody can. Nobody. Nobody. Nobody. That's why you have to smear yourself like a whore with lipstick all over your face . . . "

Eternity won't settle this moment.

I am not proud of this day and this scene. I wish it had never happened. And yet it focused me. All things that had been nameless for so long slid into sudden focus. I had wanted the truth. I had yearned for clarity. Now, at last, I held it in my hands. I stood, shaking badly, in a sweet, blazing glare of my own. Open transgression had freed me. We stared at each other, between us the whimpering child. " . . . unless you apologize . . . " cried my foe, and I cried, cuttingly: "Won't that be the day! Won't that be the day!"

Oh, how sweet it felt, that moment, that cutting of the detested umbilical cord! Up to then, I had not been in open conflict. Not with her, not with my life, not with my God. Especially not with my God. True, I visualized Him only vaguely if at all, as some kind of elder statesman, standing well above us all, passing judgment on the merits of my soul on scales designed especially for me. But when I cried: " . . . apologize for what! Long shall you wait . . . " I cut myself loose. My door to Heaven fell shut with a thud, and I relished the sound, and I relished the darkness.

Books have been written on the bleakness of the pool of sin. I stood in it, up to my knees, at that moment. Seldom had I felt the strange, intoxicating bliss that comes with wanting hard to hurt. I meant to hurt this stupid, irritating creature. And I knew as all God's little children know at such a moment, that for this feeling, for this anger, I would pay. Listen, God! That's what she is, a prattling fool! The fault is Yours—let that be known. For having made me different. For having cast me different, so You could watch small, petty minds force me into a mold that does not fit, that chokes me, deforms me, and will surely kill me in the end unless I struggle free. "That will be the day . . . " I kept on repeating, over and over, until she fled from me and up the stairs to find tearful refuge with Tina.

CHAPTER NINE

The Accident

RUDY WAS BORN on November 9, 1960. My second son was very different from my first. Erwin had been big and blond and sturdy. Rudy seemed finely chiselled, with shapely hands and narrow feet and long black hair. His face was sheerest symmetry. He yawned at me with a hearty, chest-swollen chuckle. He snuggled up against my breast and started sucking gustily. The marvel of that moment! I had forgotten that a baby could do that—swallow without effort.

I remember lying in my pillows, giddy with relief. Only now did I face up to my assorted hidden fears. I had expected to be punished. I had expected some kind of a monster—a harelip, perhaps, or a child with webbed extremities. In my burdened state of pregnancy, I had made a mountain out of a perfectly average Mennonite molehill. What was a little squabble after all in our barren lives filled by necessity with gossip, innuendo, and intrigue? Why, I would patch up our petty in-law spat. *Mutter* would weep, only too glad to forgive me. I would forgive her, too. I would draw remorse from my unwilling heart, letting bygones be bygones, and say so, as often as needed. And next time she decided to count cars from Tina's kitchen window—why, in demureness I would sit with her and keep her tally, help her guess where they might go.

I am sure a good psychiatrist could poke and probe into these musings and read meaning into them and say I had begun to bend. I had begun to blame myself for anything that an avenging Heaven might do to my innocent sons. I knew I must restrain my insolent, strident impatience with all who were slower than I, to make sure my children did not pay the penalty, for the truth was stark and plain: I did not suffer fools. I must learn to camouflage my differentness, at best a source of quiet embarrassment among my kin, at worst a constant heartache for those who must put up with me. Our script was old and fixed: I knew it all too well.

That morning, for once, I lay bathed in heavenly grace. God's ledger did not balance good and evil as a sinner might suppose. I had put myself in jeopardy, but I was worthy after all. I was forgiven, blessedly. I closed my eyes and concentrated on a prayer. I do not handle prayers well. To this day, I don't know how to pray convincingly. Somehow, my kind of prayer goes astray. That morning, I drew on fastidious manners. I said, and I meant it: "I'll try hard. I'll be humble. I'll be quiet. I'll bite my tongue, dear Lord—I will. And next time *Mutter* picks lint off of my couch and shames me in the presence of my husband . . . "

I know I slept like an angel. It did not even bother me that Woldi did not come. Well, just a little bit, perhaps, let me admit it. I knew my husband and his reasons well, but still his absence stung. He had not slept at all the night his second son was born, doing silent vigil by my side, and now he'd be asleep, no doubt. To catch up for the night shift. That's why he did not call.

Tina called and talked on the phone for a while. Tina had checked up on Kate, and now she assured me with many sweet words that Erwin was well taken care of. Kate had come in the morning and bundled him up, and had taken his bottle and diapers. No, *Mutter* had not called.

I fell weakly back into my pillows, thinking what a worry-wart I had become. It was true—I was much too protective. I had contributed to Erwin's slow development by hovering too close, by worrying too much. Now I was given three glorious days to myself to think about that, to mend my ways and be a more nonchalant Mennonite mother. Two sons! Yes, I would try. That much I could surely promise.

I smiled at my Mennonite doctor and asked: "When can I go home?" I was swimming in a gentle sea of peace. Perhaps he would say: "Why don't you stay an extra day? You look somewhat peaked . . . " I so wanted to be pampered for a change.

"Saturday," he said, patting my hand. "Aren't you lucky! Your baby is a beauty of a boy. Has your husband come by yet?"

"He works," I said, blushing.

To have work was a blessing that year when unemployment hovered in dark corners in the best of families. Thanks to an ad I had luckily spotted, Woldi now worked in a union shop—having been able to double his wages. No doubt he was putting in extra time to impress his new foreman. That's what it was—of course! I fought hard against the snake of vanity that noticed more and more the other mothers to my left and right. Deluged with satin-ribboned gifts. With dozens of cards. With bouquets of flowers. Their phones rang on and on. Their flow of visitors never abated. And here was I, every bit as good as they, with not a single visitor, with not a single present, with not a single rose. It took but little salt to make an old wound raw.

I steeled myself. Let them not pity me.

I smiled at them and shrugged my shoulders. They smiled back at me, askew.

It was galling. Did they think there was no husband in my life?

I sat in my bed, jealousy eating a hole into my joy. I knew Woldi and his diffidence in matters of the heart—but this, I decided, was simply too much: This was neglect, and well he should know it! No doubt *Mutter* had captured him deftly to drive her to a distant relative so she could spread the news about my brand new baby boy. And here I was, the star of the show, alone and forgotten. I wanted to know how Kate was managing Erwin. And I wanted to show off my new, perfect son. I marveled at the ease with which he could be handled, diapered, held—so different this child compared to struggling, thrashing Erwin.

Faintly, I heard the howl of a siren.

I picked up the phone and dialed Tina's number, guessing about the exchange. I was not at ease with the devilish thing. To this day, I do not like to use a telephone where I must verify myself to silent air as if I had no face.

Buzz. Buzz.

I tried Kate's number.

Buzz. Buzz.

With some reluctance, I dialed *Mutter's* place.

No answer.

What was going on? Where was my husband? Why didn't he call? It was unfair. It was incredible.

The siren, very near now, howled to a screeching stop below my fifth floor window. A nurse came running, ripping the receiver from my hand. I could tell by the flush in her face that something had happened, that she was upset. What had I done? Had I misdialed?

"Sorry." I opened my palms in a gesture I hoped would placate her. "I won't do it again." Since I only spoke German, my voice would have to convey the extent of good will. She talked rapidly, hanging over me. I caught a strong, unpleasant whiff of garlic. She might as well have spoken Greek. Why must she shout? I was embarrassed and ashamed—how could I tell her why it was important that I reach somebody in my extended family before another evening was gone? I looked at her with a compliant smile and repeated: "Sorry. Sorry." That was the one word I had learned.

She took me by the shoulders. She shook me hard. She

tried to tell me something, something torrential and complicated and obviously very, very urgent. Had I jammed up the telephone? Had I interfered with an emergency?

"Listen . . . " she said. "Please, you listen . . . "

I shook my head again, hoping she would go away. I could see the look of dismay and confusion pass over her face. She kept shouting something, shaking me and shaking me. She pointed to the clipboard in her hand. It was clear she wanted me to sign it. I had been amply warned by *Mutter* not to sign my name to anything, for hedonistic dangers lurked in Canadian maternity wards — commercial outfits trying to sell diaper service, glossy baby photographs, tickets to a baby contest, cribs with automatic bells. "Sorry, no." I pushed the clipboard aside and shook my head regretfully. "No. Thank you very much!" I clearly had a princely child, but I had also my realities: Christmas at my door step and not yet half of the presents bought, the second of three steep installments on our stove still due, the milkman who had waited weeks already, who any day might stop milk delivery.

She would not go away. She took my shoulders hard, repeating something, over and over, until in a slow-motion horror a meaning of sorts formed from her words: " . . . operate."

The German word is close: " . . . *operieren.*"

With a bolt, I sat upright.

No. No. No.

It couldn't be. It was impossible. I felt like Marie Antoinette, about to be beheaded for the second time. The Lord's unfailing judgment. My second child, about to be destroyed. She pointed to the clipboard, pleading with me urgently. I was to sign. Was he hurt? Was he near death? I signed with shaking fingers. With flapping skirts she scurried down the hall.

No, I won't go to hell. I have already been there.

Had a nurse dropped Rudy by mistake? Had he choked on his pillows? What had happened? Would anybody tell me, please? I kept pleading: Dear Lord. Not Rudy. Not this child—please! Anything! I will put up with anything. Just let my second son be well.

Yet all the while I knew: At last He had caught up with me. As a cat might play with a mouse, He had played with my complacency, lulling me into false hopes in a cruel pointless game whose drama now unfolded hideously: " . . . to the third and fourth generation." Where was that written? Once I had known. All along, He had schemed and plotted my demise. All along He knew how He would lay me low.

Nobody came to tell me anything. An hour passed. Two. Three. Where was my doctor? The evening crept on. The night took over slowly. My roommates had hushed. The night nurse fluffed my pillow. Midnight came, and still no one told me.

Someone gave me a pill in a tiny paper cup. I hid it under my pillow. If suffer I must, I would do so with eyes fully open, with senses sharp and clear. I believe that for all time this night changed me beyond recall. I ceased to believe in a good, just, benevolent God. I could see His plot quite clearly now. He gave so He could take away. I was helpless in the hands of such a being. For a moment of frivolity, He would calmly slay a child. For a hurtful sentence wrought from weeks of irritation, he had flung me from His grace. I listed all my sins: Disobedience. Impatience. Selfishness. Insolence. Lack of charity of heart. Yes, and this was true as well—I did not want another child. So He would let me have a glimpse, just long enough to make me fall in love with that sweet perfect cherub, and then make me bury him in a cold November grave, to teach me a critical lesson. The nurse pulled the curtains around me, entombing me with sympathy.

It was sheer hell, that night. It made me ancient.

At four o'clock in the morning, Woldi arrived. He looked ashen. He shook like a leaf. In the hush of the sleeping fifth floor, he put his dark, handsome head on my blanket. He begged: "Say no. Say no. He isn't dying, is he? Do you think that he might die?"

I was weeping also. "I don't know."

"He looks horrible. They gave him oxygen. He cannot breathe at all . . . "

"Nobody told me anything. The doctor didn't come, and I can't understand the nurses. Do you suppose that someone dropped him by mistake?"

Woldi said: "Do you . . . " and could not finish.

"Do you know what happened? Would anybody tell me what has happened, please?"

His voice broke: "They found him in convulsions. Victor called an ambulance. They put a mask on him. They drilled large holes in his temples to let the pressure out. This big . . . " He was sparing me nothing. "I've just come back from Hamilton . . . "

Hamilton? Why Hamilton? That was a city thirty miles away. Why would anyone transfer a newborn from a perfectly good hospital all the way to Hamilton?

"What . . . ?" And then it was as if a shroud were lifted from a body, and the mangled thing was not the baby I expected it to be.

It wasn't Rudy who was hurt. It was Erwin.

Slowly, details dripped into my brain. Kate hadn't watched him. Kate had been busy gossiping. She had left him crawling, and Erwin had toddled among neighborhood children watching TV, children bigger and rougher than Erwin, impatient with him. Erwin had not kept away; he had tried to haul himself up on a knob, distorting their picture, blocking their view. They had tried to lift him on a chair, and he had slipped, had fallen backwards. He had hit his head—on what? A toy? A planter? Kate didn't know. Kate was hysterical, too. All Kate knew was that she found him senseless. She tried to shake him hard, but shaking him had done no good—"That's when they came to look for me . . . " said Woldi.

"I heard the sirens," I said, over and over, as if such trivia mattered now. "They stopped in front of my window . . . "

"He's dying," said Woldi. "I know it. He's dying. Is he going to die? Say no. Say no."

CHAPTER TEN

Nightmare

I CHECKED MYSELF OUT of the hospital as soon as the morning shift nurses opened their files. I sat, silent and subdued, in the back of Victor's car, weak from loss of blood and medication. As if through a blanketing fog, I heard Victor pleading with Woldi: " . . . she shouldn't go . . . she shouldn't go . . . why don't we take her home . . . ?" and Woldi's voice that answered somewhere in the universe: " . . . well, don't you know she doesn't listen . . . "

We drove from one hospital straight to the next. We pulled into the parking lot. Victor kept pleading: " . . . in her condition . . . " and Woldi turned to me " . . . in your condition . . ." and I said sharply: " . . . shut up, both of you, and help me up those stairs . . . "

A maze of halls smelled once again of medicine — the now familiar smell of ether that hit me like a fist. Then I stood, my newborn in my arms, and looked at Erwin, speechless.

This was my child?

He sat motionless and stiff, propped up by half a dozen pillows. His skull was shaven. Thick gauze was wrapped around his head. His body was stripped of all clothing. His skin looked mottled and blue. All around him in his crib lay heavy open ice packs. They were freezing my baby to death! Deep surgical gashes had opened both of his ankles. Embedded in the bloody cuts lay long needles attached to plastic tubes that wound around his bed. Out of his left nostril ran another, thicker tube, taped to his cheek and neck. Out of his right, a streak of crusted blood curled in a halfmoon to his ear. Black, crusted blood on his lips, on his fingers. A heap of bloody gauze beneath his crib. He sat, stiff and blue, as if the ice bags had frozen him to his pillows. My baby's eyes were wide open. My baby's eyes were dead.

Not a doctor, not a nurse was in sight.

I can only vaguely recall the next hour or two. Victor spoke a little English, but not enough to help us out. We could not ask a single question. In the end, I pulled an old grocery receipt from Woldi's pocket and wrote down my landlord's telephone number. My fingers were floating in space. "Please," I wrote in awkward German, "if he worsens, call me at once." I pinned that to Erwin's crib. I made it back to our car. Victor drove. Woldi kept his face averted. In my lap slept Rudy, peacefully.

Kate was waiting for me in my kitchen. So was *Mutter,* starting to wail as soon as I stepped through the door. I pushed them both away. It felt like a punch into cotton. Through a haze I saw them floating as they both bent over Rudy, weeping loudly, assuring me over and over that I had, by far, the most beautiful child in the world. I said to poor Kate: "Shut up, you stupid slut!" and to *Mutter* I said thickly, for my tongue was no longer my own: "For as long as I live, I will never ask of you another favor." I don't remember the rest of the day. I don't remember what Woldi and I said to each other. I was drowned in tranquilizers and the deep despair of knowing, knowing, knowing that our worries had not ceased by coming here to Canada. Our troubled journey with our damaged son had barely begun.

The faint ring of the telephone awakened me. I was alone

in my bedroom except for that small, stirring bundle next to me. I could see that it was almost dark outside. Woldi must have left for work after packing me with some pillows. Through the thick walls, I could hear the telephone. Relentless. Menacing.

Ring.

Ring.

Our landlord had partitioned off our apartment from the rest of the cellar. There was a door from our kitchen to his storage space, and from there a staircase led to his kitchen. He opened that door once a week to let me use his washing machine. At other times, he kept it closed. He was a most suspicious man, guarding his assorted treasures: door frames, rusty hinges, sinks, cupboards, tiles, a doorless freezer — things he had salvaged from wrecking old homes. That door was locked and bolted now, and apparently no one at home!

It must be Hamilton!

It had to be.

The phone kept ringing.

It stopped. It rang again.

I tried to force open the door. No give. I stood, panting, telling myself: It might be some gossip. Some salesman. Why, it could be just anyone.

Ring. Ring.

It did not stop ringing — it kept on and on. I knew my landlord's habits well. Never did his phone ring that persistently.

I felt as if a hand were slowly choking me as I tried to force open the door with a knife. Clearly, this was an emergency call. Another signature was needed. Erwin had worsened. He was dying. He was dead. What did they do with dead babies here in this cold, incomprehensible, frightening land?

I began, with what strength I had left, to throw myself against the door to break it down. I took a pillow for a cushion, held it to my shoulder, tried again. Something on the other side gave way; the door flew open with a thud. I climbed over toasters, waffle irons, broken TV sets, old radios, feeling for the light switch. I saw with relief that the door at the top of the staircase was open. There was the phone. I lunged for it: *"Hallo . . . ?"*

The party hung up.

Immediately it rang again.

Again I said, more forcefully: *"Hallo? Hallo?"*

Nothing but a startled silence at the other end.

"Ola . . . ?" I said, shaking, remembering my Spanish. " . . . Baby? Hamilton?"

The person on the other line slammed down the receiver.

Barely had I put mine down when the devilish thing jumped again in an ear-splitting ring.

Oh, God. What now?

I ran back down the stairs, grabbed my sleeping baby, wrapped him tightly in the largest blanket I could find. The front door flew out of my hands in the howling winds of November. The desperation of that night made me remember, suddenly, a German import store. I had seen it in passing, and now, in my need, I even remembered the street, but how could I find it? A *landsmann* would know what to do. Ring. Ring. The sound drove me into the wind, into the darkness. Ring. Ring.

Ring.

Ring.

I started walking, asking people: *"Deutscher Laden?"* German store? Few understood me. Some pointed left. Some pointed right. Some shook their heads, not comprehending. A woman, retrieving an evening paper from out of the bushes, saw me standing in the wind, shivering and weeping, and took me by the arm. "Hansa Import? Sure."

Bless her soul. She put me in her car, started a sputtering motor, and, spewing smoke and gravel, took me there.

Someone handed me a cup of hot, delicious tea. Someone patted my shoulder. I just sat and sipped and shook. Someone dialed the hospital in Hamilton for me. Erwin was still comatose. Yes, the situation was unchanged.

Yes, Ma'm. The doctor would call.

No, there was nothing anyone could do.

Thank you. Thank you. Thank you.

The owners of the Hansa Import said: "We'll keep our line open for any emergency calls. We will let you know at once — we promise. Let us now take you home. Would you like to take along this old hot water bottle? How about another piece of cake? How old is that beautiful baby? Two weeks? Three weeks?

"Two days," I told them, teeth chattering.

They drove me home. They put me to bed. They diapered my baby and put him next to me. Barely had they left, and barely had I closed my eyes when my landlord, livid with anger, woke me again. Break and enter — didn't I know? The cat had escaped. And the door was scratched disgracefully. He should have listened to his friends. His friends had warned him many times against the unreliability of immigrants. Against his better instincts he had taken us in, to give us a chance, to do us a Christian favor — but were we duly grateful? No! Union people already! Too ignorant to know that anybody had to work his way up from the bottom and sweat it out with little jobs for many, many years!

I stuttered: " . . . the telephone rang . . . "

There was an explanation to the relentless telephone, and that was, indirectly, on my conscience, too. Hadn't he given us work out of sheer kindness, hoping that we would stay with him for awhile for low pay? Didn't I know about unions — that they were run by Communists? Hundreds had called, in response to his ad, grateful to find honest work from an honest, struggling private enterprise. Would I please inform my husband that, as of today, our rent was raised $10.00 to pay for restoring the door?

CHAPTER ELEVEN

Seven Lost Years

WE LIVED FOR SEVEN YEARS in Canada. Charred holes remain where memory should be. I remember bits and pieces of the early and mid-Sixties, but I can't claim comprehensive knowledge of those years. I believe that through some weird design of time warp, in the end I learned to survive by forgetting the worst, but along with the pain I erased, I erased much that was wondrous as well.

I don't remember Rudy, for example, as a baby very clearly. I have mental glimpses of him that I cherish—a wispy child in his first yellow snowsuit, a dimpled toddler on a swing, a four-year-old precocious youngster on his first stout walk to school. Those memories tug at my heart. He was like a bonus of beauty—in all respects a perfect child. I should have memorized his first sweet words, recorded them in frilly baby books. I should have seen him grow and develop, and known pride in his well-focused mind. I should have formed that inner bond so tenuous in later years that makes for a lifelong parent-child union. In my haze of despair and fatigue, all this was quite out of reach. Erwin usurped me.

Erwin lived in a world where every sight, every sound of

everyday living was painful bombardment that threw my child into a screaming, howling, baying, twitching, unrelenting pain. It was like living with a stick of dynamite, like living on the thinnest razor edge of absolute exhaustion, like having fallen deep into a pit of poison ivy, bound hands and feet. There was no relaxing with Erwin around—a speck of dust, a sudden word, a squeaking door could send him on a rampage.

I have some answers today why this was so, but how I wish I had had answers then—what a difference it would have made! Erwin's brain received too many signals; he could not sort them out. His tolerance threshold was exceedingly frail—any sight, sound, or smell could shatter his fragile resources. In simplest terms, learning to live and adjust, for any normal child, means processing these raw sensations by means of tiny batteries located in the brain. Periodically, these batteries discharge and re-charge themselves by complex chemical means to create some intricate meaning: "This is a window." "Listen to this word." "Repeat after me." "Give me your hand."

Simple instructions? Not for an injured mind. My baby was besieged with sensations.

A normal child will filter out the essence of the concept "window," for example. A window is a pane of glass, part of a room, no more. This definition is implied, it's matter-of-fact, it's taken for granted. A normal child will integrate the concept "window" into his overall repertoire of things he has already learned. He stores it; he puts it out of sight. He can leave it alone until such time when he has some use for it. He is not likely to react to a window beyond its functional, taken-for-granted properties. It is there. It *is*. He is hardly aware of its presence.

In a brain-injured child's tormented world, a window is an ever-present irritant, incomprehensible and menacing. It will not leave him alone, no matter how he fights and squirms and raves and twists to protect himself against the onslaught of sensations he can't handle or assemble: the curtains move, flies buzz against the pane, trees bend to air he cannot see and therefore cannot comprehend, cars swish by and these cars buzz and roar and blare and screech and honk, pedestrians appear and disappear without the slightest rhyme or reason, and so do tricycles and roller skates and motor bikes—nothing, nothing is constant! A normal brain discards irrelevant input as useless, as trivia. A damaged brain cannot. Evolution made the human brain insensitive to anything not of immediate, practical use. Brain damage undoes that. A hurt brain remains overwhelmed. It cannot help its weird commands. It simply must explode. It has no choice but to explode. Anything can set it off, nothing can contain it.

Erwin's faulty brain cells forced him to pay attention to all stimuli with screaming, howling, spinning, biting fury. Before his injury at Kate's, he had been such a restless, floppy, whiny child. He came back to us from Hamilton a raving, raging freak.

His mind would all but collapse from trying to accommodate the countless trivial "memories." Erwin could neither assemble, nor could he forget—he simply lacked adequate filters. At the mercy of a furious firestorm of electrical signals, his entire body overheated in my untutored hands to sheer convulsing agony. Anything could do it, bring it on: a missing picture on the wall, unexpected company, the unaccustomed smell of certain spices I might try, the tick-tick-ticking of a clock we had foolishly purchased, a car that would not start, or did.

Even then I understood that what I saw before me must have a molecular, chemical reason. Sweat would pour in salty rivulets from his entire body as I watched him spin and whoop and bay and howl in a vain attempt to shake the noxious stimuli that wrought such havoc with his mind.

It was sheer hell on earth to live with such a child.

Much of what we know today of the architecture of the brain, of the multi-faceted activities of enzymes involved in sending out impulses, has come to us within the past ten, fifteen years. I am convinced that answers for relief from stimulus bombardment must come from biochemistry. Some progress, I am told, is being made. Scientists continue to search for a chemical way to coat and to channel the raw nervous energy that makes its victims " . . . climb the walls . . . " as folklore aptly puts it. My child not only climbed the walls, he walked on my ceiling, he stomped on my soul, he shredded my patience, he ravaged my heart, he killed my youth.

How many times was I admonished:
" . . . not a trace of discipline . . . !"
" . . . can't you try to calm him down . . . ?"
" . . . is there no way to make him mind . . . ?"

Can the chaotic world of one's dreams be controlled? Have you tried to run and fight when you are bolted to the floor? Erwin bit and kicked and screamed and spun in circles at my feet — for years! He chewed up my newspaper and ripped apart my tablecloth and devoured my plants — leaves, roots and all. He would chew on his fingers and lips until they were bloody, or gnaw on his nails until they were gone.

Here are some of the objects he swallowed: beads, buttons, coins, matches, fruit pits, pebbles, rubber bands, safety pins, shoelaces. The simplest act of feeding him was a domestic battle, leaving gobs of cereal on the floor, spaghetti plastered to the wall, my wrists full of punctures where he had dug his nails and teeth into my flesh. I would put him in his crib — about the only place where I would know him free of harm — and he would grasp the rails and rock it through the house and follow me about — a wild-eyed, howling monster. He broke every dish that he could reach, hurling them across the room with fury and with vengeance. He slept as if he were coiled, springing to wild swipes and grabs at the slightest unaccustomed movement in the room. When he was little, his hearing was sharply acute. He could " . . . hear the grass grow . . . " as they say, and hearing grass grow, for my child, was torture. In later years, he lost much of his hearing — he "tuned out," the doctors said. I am sure he turned deaf in self-defense — it hurt too much to hear. When he would fall asleep, exhausted, somewhere in a corner, we all collapsed with him. It seems to me the only time I spoke to Rudy in those early years would be to hiss: "Shhhh! Erwin is asleep! Be quiet! Don't wake him up!!!"

What a life!

Oh, for the luxury of even half a cup of coffee with a neighbor! I did not know that simple joy for years. I would do my dishes with one hand, fiercely trying to control Erwin with the other. Once I tried to iron some shirts while doing furious battle with my knees, trying to keep him from strangling himself with the long extension cord. Somehow he managed to grab it and pull it apart, and before I could stop him, he had put his tongue to the wire. The current sent him reeling, and thereby, painfully, he learned his first meaningful word.

"Hot!"

I picked him up and shook my howling misfit: "Hot! No! Hot! No!" I kept repeating the two words over and over. In those years, I knew nothing about the principles of learning, but instinctively I did what must be done to words to make them acquire meaning: I paired the emotional content of one word with the meaning of another yet unknown. "Hot means No! No means limits!"

This gave me an anchor of sorts—the tiniest flicker of hope. If he could learn two words and know their meanings, surely with time and patience he could come to master four. Four could be doubled to eight. Eight to sixteen. More than enough for a meaningful sentence. I could double one sentence to two, and two to four, and so on, until he could listen and reason. I never forgot this beginning, though "hot" and "no" remained the only words he knew for many years. He had no language, poor thing, and therefore he could not store meaning.

In this devilish, chaotic world, Rudy grew up without effort. How could that be? I marvel at it even now, at the ease with which he spoke, at the ease with which his eyes could follow me. This second child simply unfolded and blossomed, and not a thing for me to do!

In no time at all my little, black-eyed second son managed an unswerving line from here to there. He learned to hop and skip. He learned to ride a bike. He strolled about the house with real, determined purpose and soon moved about the neighborhood. Rudy could jump in one place. Rudy could hop on alternate feet. Wonder of wonders, Rudy could tiptoe!

Erwin did not master walking backwards until he was well over ten years of age.

Rudy was a child of boundless energy and vigor, endowed with a rich and vivid mind. He would raise his arms to help me dress him — why, I never knew that children could do that! Rudy would carry my dust pan, wanting to make himself useful. Erwin, always underfoot, would for certain land — head first — in one of my detergent pails, don't ask me how, or how often. I could hold and comfort Rudy. Erwin was impossible to soothe when he was hurt. Rudy cried real tears — little perfect drops that rolled symmetrically from a symmetric face. Erwin's face distorted grossly; tears pushed out from every pore — blistering, menacing things, spreading all over his forehead, all over his temples and cheeks and neck and into his hair. On his sturdy, dimpled legs, Rudy started valiant excursions deep into the orchards that surrounded our streets. Erwin clutched onto my skirts for years. Rudy fabricated new expressions, and those words were words of clarity and purpose. Erwin, using the few utterances he learned to master over time, sounded like a screeching, broken record. Rudy was a compact personality. Erwin's psyche seemed a blob.

I can't remember ever seeing Erwin smile when he was very young. He must have. I have some old snapshots that tell me he did. I find that unbelievable. I only recall: every day, every week, every month and every year took me deeper into a tunnel from which there was no release, no reprieve, no return.

In those years, I know today, I came close to knowing madness. What does it mean to go insane? I never saw or heard odd things. I never battled voices. I never was locked up, or put on medication, or analyzed, nor did I ever tell a soul. But I am sure today that I was very, very ill.

CHAPTER TWELVE

Madness

TIME WAS DISTORTING. I noticed that first. I could no longer tell the seasons of the year, much less the day of the week or the time of the day without a major mental effort. I hid that knowledge from my family. It would have drained my energy to bother to explain.

Every once in a while, I felt a sweet yearning to hurt. This yearning, as yet, had no focus. But I knew it was there. Its presence swept me like a flame, and when it seared me, now and then, it gave me brief relief.

I severed all relations with my in-laws. That was easy. That was a cinch.

"Let bygones be bygones . . . " *Mutter* would plead, and I would look at my child: " . . . what bygones?"

"To your God you have to answer, not to me . . . " she would wail, and I would replace the receiver and look out of the window and feel my conscience wash over with mudslides of grey. Was there a God? Why had He singled me out? Why had He struck his blow so viciously? What had I done—just what? to deserve this?

" . . . it's never too late to repent," *Mutter* would weep, and I would listen, numb and alone, aghast at the obscenity of a small mind that dared translate my tragedy into a distant victory for God.

"I'm through with them," I said.

"We don't have to see them any more," said Woldi, "if it upsets you so to have them visit us. Although, for the life of me, I can't see why you're always upset . . . "

I am sure that Woldi must have suffered, too. He did his part. He did what he could, but it did not suffice. I was no longer reachable. He worked long, life-sapping hours, and I would write check after check to pay off our staggering medical bills. He slaved through many hours working overtime all through our years in Canada, but never once did he sit down and talk to me and put a kind word to a hideous wound.

On Sundays he went fishing.

He did not live my hell. He did not like to hear of it. "What do you want?" he would ask, exasperated. Wasn't I proud of the home we had purchased, proud of the things that I owned? My ice box? My washer-dryer? My TV?

There was no comfort in his touch, no feeling of belonging, only a sorrow, deep and forlorn. What had happened to our love? I would grit my teeth and swallow my nausea and count to one hundred, hoping and praying that what must be done would still leave me breathing, would not extinguish my last quivering shred of existence. I learned to endure the brutal moments that come when all longings and feelings are gone.

Erwin was three, Rudy a year-and-a-half when I found out, too deep in shock to weep, that yet another child was on the way. I did not say a word to anyone. If I opened my mouth, a sea of resentment would drown me.

There came the day when I struck Erwin, sending him reeling the length of the room. I don't remember just why—in all likelihood in response to a small, insignificant matter. Perhaps I could no longer tolerate his lurch? What do I know? Others have struck a child with less provocation than I.

Afterwards, I took him in my arms and tried to summon some shred, some semblance of feeling of shame. His anguish was greater than mine. I knew that. I put my hands to his face. He was running a fever. I sat rocking him, withdrawn into some hollow well of loneliness, thinking with detachment that in my ghastly slow disintegration I could no longer tell between the torments of his body and my own.

I had struck him, but it was I who sat, hurting in every last cell of my body.

I sat and held him to me and tried to ride it out, this ungodly pain that had no focus and no name and no beginning and no end, that swept me in wave after wave. "Sit still," I said. "Oh, please. Sit still for just a minute . . ." But Erwin could never be held for any length of time—he clawed at me and tried to sink his teeth into my hand and so I let him go. As I bent to put him on the floor, I felt my back go into spasms. In a matter of seconds I was in such pain I did not think I could live. I sat, doubled over, within a solid white-hot flame. When it let up, I managed to lift him. I managed to restrain him long enough to put him in his crib. He howled in protest and fury and rammed his teeth into the metal bars.

I stumbled outside, calling for Rudy. I found him playing in the sand box. "Come on," I said. "You have to go to bed. Right now." It was still early afternoon.

I took him by the hand and felt my way across the steps, now blinded by a pain beyond compare. I put him in his crib as well. I made it to my bed. I even managed to pull off the blankets. It was as if demons befell me. My bed was soaked with blood and sweat—apt evidence that demons had their way with me.

Through waves of agony I heard both children scream. There was nothing whatsoever I could do—I could not move at all, for if I tried a single step, that would be the end of me.

The afternoon trickled away.

There was no doubt. My pregnancy had ended. Luckily.

This thing on my sheets, this mass of fiber and jelly, should have been a child. There was a little head, the size and texture of a prune. It lay, collapsed into itself, in the bloody hollow of my palm, flabby and limp, the size of a mouse.

Rudy was quiet now. Erwin continued to scream.

By late afternoon, I lifted myself from my rack. I felt my way along the hall, holding onto chairs and door knobs, like a criminal dripping with blood. I opened the door. Rudy had fallen asleep from exhaustion. He lay on the edge of his pillow, rosy of cheek and fully at peace. Erwin stood there like an evil dervish, fistfuls of fiber and foam hanging from his mouth. He had torn all clothing from his body. He had ripped his plastic mattress into shreds. He had badly hurt himself on the sharp exposed metal springs—there was blood, and there were feces. There were bloody feces simply everywhere. I looked at him and did not think I could survive another hour of this madness, much less another day.

Parents of handicapped children get brisk professional scoldings for "going from doctor to doctor" in a foolish, vain search for relief. We did that, too—we went doctor-shopping with a vengeance. We paid many hundreds of doctors to label the horror we had on our hands. Aphasia. Ataxia. Cranial nerve palsy. Organic brain damage. Autism. Dysphasia. Expressive disorders. Erwin's childhood bulged with professional tags. Doctors freely helped themselves by copying from each other. Never once did any doctor think it expedient to take a few minutes to sit down with me and explain just what it all meant.

Perhaps they assumed that I knew. Perhaps they took it for granted that I grasped the struggle that life had handed me. I did not. I had not the faintest idea. I thought my baby was possessed—as punishment for my assorted sins.

I did not, in the early Sixties, speak English very well and had no way of learning it, since I seldom left my home. I might go out to do some hurried shopping, but that was the extent of my excursions into the English-speaking world. Judiciously, I avoided my non-Mennonite neighbors. And since I had broken all relations with the Mennonites—and they with me—I was alone, marked on the forehead, for all the world to see.

I found I could no longer talk to anyone. Silence was my harbor of escape, my secret corner into which to crawl, my private haven where I could shut the door. I stood behind a glass partition. "They" could see me, but "they" could not touch or hurt me any more.

The only English-speaking person that befriended me in those years was an elderly public health nurse who had come to visit when Rudy was a baby. She kept in loose touch with me through the years, dropping in whenever she had business to attend to in my part of town, sitting on my couch to catch a breath of air, fiddling with her notebook. I liked her well enough. We made clumsy conversation: "Beautiful day." "Going to snow." Once or twice I tried to talk to her about my fears for Erwin: "Old baby ill. Young baby fine." My English was an awkward thing; it did not stretch at all.

I remember one conversation that was to haunt me afterwards for many years to come.

"What does he eat?" she wanted to know, pad on her knees, pencil neatly poised.

"Doughnuts," I said proudly. That my child, at four, could now eat doughnuts without gagging was a major victory. He had an abnormal craving for sugar; almost all the food he ate was very sweet. I tried to accommodate him, glad there was something I could do to give him at least some small joy. That week I had bought a dozen sugar doughnut cartons at a special baker's sale. I opened my refrigerator. "All day long," I told her proudly, "he eats doughnuts."

She scribbled that into her notebook. Her comment was to follow me for years through countless doctors' offices: "This child looks badly malnourished. His mother only feeds him doughnuts . . . " I am still bitter about that remark — it was so unfair and untrue.

Nobody knew how to offer help or advice. Nobody told me that there was therapy, or tests, or early schools perhaps, or medication such as tranquilizers. Once I buttonholed a doctor after Erwin crushed a finger in a door jamb: "What can I do? How can I control him . . . ?"

The young, handsome doctor stood by the door, hands in his coat, impatient to leave, letting me guess by piecing some meaning together from snatches of incomprehensible words: " . . . damaged brain cells . . . no reversal . . . can't be changed."

"Pills?"

"No. I'm sorry."

"Tests?"

He shook his head. Why test? Tests were expensive and painful. But had I ever talked to someone in Toronto? At the Children's Hospital? Would I want that? For understanding? Clarity? "Look at my hand," said the good doctor, spreading five well-manicured fingers. "If I lost it after birth, would that be so different from having been born without a hand to begin with?" What difference would it make to know just how it happened? It happened. That was that.

From the depths of my being I pried loose my own resolution as many parents will: "That doctor is wrong. What's more, I will prove it. Just watch what I will do to prove that phony doctor wrong . . . " Parents have to do it. It is normal, I believe. It is therapeutic. Let one who never walked in our shoes cast that first stone. To say to the professional: " . . . you're wrong" serves as a vent; it is said for a purpose. For parents, it is a compelling reaction to long and unbearable stress.

What next? Well, for a start, I could put science over prayers. Scientific evidence as to the "when" and "how" would give me an anchoring start. Once and for all, I would find out.

Was there a clot in Erwin's brain? Scarred tissue? Could he see? Could he hear? And what about his flat-bridged nose, his double-jointed fingers? And just how did it happen? Was it the jungle surgery? Was it that he almost starved to death because of his paralyzed throat muscles? Was it the horrid fall that cracked his skull from ear to ear, that left him ten days in a coma? I would get my answers. I was mad for action, wanting things done.

I remember the day we went to Toronto to the Children's Hospital. Surely the doctors there would do a little more than tap his knees and shine a beam of light into his eyes and tickle his spastic footsoles? I braced myself for an extended diagnostic stay. I was determined that, English or not, I would squeeze guidance and direction out of every snatch of wisdom. I bought a simple dictionary to fortify myself: "What treatment?" "What program?" "What school?"

We were led into the doctor's office. A brisk little nurse tried to undress my terrified offspring, only to yelp and flee from the room. His teeth were sharp, his terror boundless.

"What's wrong?" the doctor bellowed.

That's why I had come. That's what I wanted to know.

"What *is* wrong?" I whispered. I stared at him. He glared at me. Woldi sat, legs outstretched, to show that nothing would shock him. I sensed that he was greatly frightened, too.

The good doctor rose with a sigh. With distaste, he studied Erwin's bitten fingers. He rapped his chest. He took his rubber hammer to tap him on his knees. Tap-tap. Tap-tap. Twice on each side. Others had done this before him. He tickled his footsoles, as others had done. He told me, as others had told me: "There is absolutely nothing I can do." He said: "If I were you, I'd put him away, what with this beautiful youngster you have here . . . " He ruffled Rudy's hair. He jovially turned to Woldi: " . . . well, now. Don't *you* agree . . . ?" He wrote to a colleague: " . . . my feelings with these silent parents are that institutionalization would be best, but I emphasized to them that this was a decision they themselves would have to make . . . "

The Niagara Peninsula, a blooming orchard paradise, seemed one gigantic funeral to me. When a normal child dies, flowers and cards, letters and prayers are seemly. Concern and sympathy are offered lavishly, welcomed by the grieving souls to help them come to terms with loss. The ritual of grief marks death with a finality that helps a parent to let go. For our kind of loss, there were no words of comfort, there was no ritual. Our child had died in mind if not in body. We drove, alone, through clouds of incense. Endlessly.

CHAPTER THIRTEEN

The Search

STRONG ARE THE MYTHS about mothers. They say a mother can move mountains, and so I thought it must be true. I resolved I would move them. I started to write.

"Dear Ann Landers . . . " I wrote. Dear Columnist. Dear Famous Doctor. Dear University.

Somebody sent me three names — a beginning. I wrote to all three the very next day. They, in turn, sent other names. I wrote to them all. I had my marching orders now. I wrote letter after letter. John F. Kennedy was shot, and Jack Ruby gunned down Oswald, and it was said that there was something " . . . wrong with Ruby's brain." I traced the man who would trace Ruby's brain waves. His name was Frederick Gibbs; he practiced in Chicago. He who knew scientific facts enabling him to tell a killer from a victim would surely know a way to help a little boy.

Professor Gibbs wrote me a very warm, personal letter. His own son had suffered permanent hearing nerve damage. Regrettably, nerve damage could not be undone. But perhaps the University of Buffalo . . .

Several times I wrote to Pearl S. Buck, who had written many years before *The Girl Who Never Grew*.

"I know that you will find a way," this sweet old lady told me, her own struggle decades behind her. "I am afraid I cannot tell you how, but I sense your strong determination in your letter . . . "

Once I stole a magazine from a dentist's office, too shy to ask if I could take it home. It listed fifty specialists. I wrote to them all. My fingers cramped. My eyes blurred. I could no more have stopped myself than I could have kept a cloud from raining, for if I stopped, I stood belted by black waves that would drown me in despair. So I wrote, and I hoped, and I kept myself precariously balanced on a crest of meager hope.

I did not know it then, but I was amassing my basics. This clumsy first correspondence taught me two things very clearly: I needed to learn to speak proper English to make myself understood, and I needed to gain intellectual distance from my grief. To summarize it differently, I had to make myself understood in a more controlled, logical, calm, articulate way. In order to reach that objective, I must know, fully and squarely, the precise nature of my child's bedeviled, weird affliction in its medical and psychological entirety. Once I had a grasp on that, I would find a way out of my guilt-ridden morass.

Thus I began to lay the groundwork for what I wanted most in later years: to become a writer of substance, and to become a well-informed psychologist.

I have forgotten by what means I chanced upon an address that simply electrified me: the famous Freiburg Children's Clinic in the Black Forest Hills of Germany.

I was too young to have known Germany at all except for a few years of war and its cold and hungry aftermath, but I still identified with being "German." Why had I not thought of this option before? If this earth held a place that could give Erwin help, that place must be in Germany.

For once, I could write straight from my heart. "Dear Doctor," I wrote in my awkward, stilted High German, "you must surely think me forward asking you . . . "

A reply came at once. Yes, there was help. Tests must be run. Three weeks, at the very least, would be needed. Three long pages, bearing all kinds of detailed instructions, promised all I dared to hope.

I trembled with relief. A load dropped from my shoulders. Costs? They were high. Staggering. Woldi and I, our bank book between us, tried to plot a strategy. We had some paltry savings, enough to pay round trip for me, but not a penny more. "But if I keep him in my lap, and since it is only one-way . . . "

I was determined for Erwin it would be one-way. I would leave him to be cured in Germany.

Woldi agreed. "I will gladly work double time." I hugged him hard. I, too, would find a job. We would trim our life to the meagerest essentials. Meatless meals. No idle rides on Sundays. Woldi kept saying: " . . . take all we have. Let's try to borrow a couple of hundred . . . " I could see that he had suffered, too. We put our arms around each other. Together, we had been through war. We said to each other: "A doctor who knows what he's doing. A modern, up-to-date clinic . . . " I could feel myself breathing again. Woldi rocked me in his arms and told me he would get a raise—why, he would just look his boss straight in the eye and simply ask for one.

I told myself he had matured. He stayed willingly with me at home now, spurning former Paraguayan buddies showing up with fishing poles. He whistled a lot. He washed out the cellar. He painted the steps. He fenced our yard with a fancy ornamental railing. He took Rudy swimming, and he willingly piggybacked Erwin for long, happy walks on the beach. He sprouted a few distinguished grey hairs. I teased him about it. "He made us old before our time," I said, and found that I could smile. For so long, I had existed in a clammy fog. Now it was lifting finally.

"Not so," said Woldi daringly.

Before another month had passed, I knew I was pregnant again.

This time I would manage. By golly, I would! I would be careful with myself and with my brand new baby. I would not let the poison of my past destroy this new life, too.

Woldi said: "Shouldn't we have *Mutter* over for a weekend?"

Much bitterness was still between us. There were choking, tearful accusations on the telephone. We feuded hard, as Mennonites are wont to do. We claim feuds that have endured the centuries, that started with small, insignificant matters, feuds that have fractured the Lord's very church, and nobody any the wiser. And mine was no small, insignificant grudge. I quivered at the touch of soul. Need the accident have happened, I wanted to know, clutching hard onto the phone, had *Mutter* been willing to lend me a hand?

Why not apologize? she wanted to know. And have a big jolly reunion?

Slam! went the receiver. There simply was no use.

The night before my scheduled departure, my in-laws descended on me to get to the bottom of my latest contrivance. Was it true that I was planning, wickedly, to take my child to Germany?

"What if he dies in Germany?" wailed *Mutter,* loudly and beseechingly. "And how come you made your plans in such secrecy?" Why was she always left out of family matters? Why was she never consulted—not once? She was girded with no excess baggage: right was right, and wrong was wrong, and what I planned was clearly wrong, and she was here to tell me! She took my wrist for emphasis. "Come here," she said. "Let's go and talk in privacy." I felt myself grow dizzy. I yanked my hand away. She cried: " . . . no Mennonite ever . . . " and I said: "To hell with all the Mennonites!" I cried, clutching onto the table: "How come I'm not a Mennonite? Just tell me that! Can you? If He likes Mennonites so much, why did he make me different? You listen to me. I'm different. I live according to different rules. My rules decree that I must take my child to Germany. . . "

It was getting dark. Victor and Kate, Albert and Tina sat in stiff silence, hoping for me to turn on the light. Well, let them sit and wait—I would not throw the switch; a sinner is safer in darkness. In the dark, I felt myself going to pieces, like a shiny drop of mercury that's splattered on the floor. I knew that pain. It reached all the way to the roots of my teeth. I put my hand on my belly to calm the spasms there. *Mutter* sat, weeping softly, in my kitchen. *Mutter* sobbed: " . . . people talk . . . " and Woldi echoed helplessly: " . . . yes, people talk, but she will only . . . " and Victor and Kate and Albert and Tina said nothing, sitting like accusing shadows, trying hard to stare me down.

All in all, we stayed married twenty years, to the dot and to the day. But that night I knew for certain and forevermore that the cord spun out of youth and love and innocence was severed. It could have been different. He could have elected to stand by my side.

He came, long after the clan had departed, and sat on the edge of my bed. He said, with some surprise: "Why, you are crying . . . " and then, after another half hour or so: " . . . well, what does it really matter? What does it matter *what* they say . . . "

I lay in the dark and stared at the ceiling. I said: "Why not one word in my defense?" and Woldi said mildly and patiently: "Well, don't you know how stubborn they can be . . . ?"

We lay beside each other, wordlessly, and after a while, I felt his hand in the small of my back. I loathed the touch. I was done with all that sick-love treachery. I knew by the familiar cramps that burrowed deep within me that this new life would not be. I would lose it again. In fact, I knew that loss to be imminent now. But I had purchased two tickets with the sweat of five years, and if I gave way to my body's revolt, I would lose my reservations. Knives of fire scraped along my spine, but I put my teeth to the corner of my pillow, willing myself to last through the night.

CHAPTER FOURTEEN

The Journey

SUITCASE IN ONE HAND, Erwin's knotted fingers in the other, I walked along the airport ramp. Woldi said awkwardly: " . . . did you give him his pill?" and I said: "Yes. Yes, I did . . . " and then we both fell silent, for there was nothing left to say.

After a very long pause:

"He seems pretty calm. Don't you agree?"

"He's not. Just look at him. He's soaking wet already . . . " Erwin's cotton shirt stuck to his shoulder blades. His forehead had furrowed. His palm lay wet in my own. Darts of lightning, I surmised, flashed between his temples. He was gnashing his teeth, about to become a Frankenstein monster.

"Give him another pill."

"I will."

"Well, then. Good luck." My husband bent and kissed me awkwardly, as modern passengers, he knew, in modern airports do. I saw him turn and leave. I was relieved to see him go. Erwin moaned softly, his head in my lap. I could sense that his brain had started to simmer. I knew it was at boiling point the moment we filed into the airplane. He had begun to swat himself. Two or three passengers stared. I pulled him along. He stiffened. I pushed. He hissed at me like a snake. I whispered exhortations.

"Come on, now—come on!"

The air was chill. I felt chill after chill in my back, in my chest, in my bones. I struggled with him down the aisle. He kicked me in the shin. I said: "Please, Erwin, please . . . " and he let fly with his first godawful howl. I faced a row of passengers. They stared at me, embarrassed and pained. My face turned red. I tried to find my seat. I attempted to wrestle him into the cushions. Fate would have it that it was a window seat—right in front of him propellers started whirring. Scarlet of face, he stared at the spinning discs. Beads of sweat had collected absolutely everywhere. I saw his eyes go out of focus.

"Please, *Schatzi* . . . "

He held his breath. His nose started bleeding. I searched for a tissue and couldn't find one. I wiped him with the corner of my blouse, for fear that he would stain the seat. I tried to shield his vision from the onslaught of the whirring propellers, his ears from the roar of the turboprop engines. I could feel his temples pounding in my hand—the hiss of the airplane went right through his surgical scars. He threw himself backwards, eyes bulging, face twisted, a child on the rack. He flung his arms about and shrieked and shrieked and shrieked—a brain on fire, literally.

" . . . baby, listen . . . "

The stewardess came running. She tried to reach for him to calm him down. He sank his teeth into her wrist. She grabbed him with quick expertise. He writhed free with overwhelming effort. Sweat poured from every pore. His head flopped about in the grip of a terror the depth of which I could only surmise. Demons were urging him on. By now, no human voice could reach him.

"Does he have to go?" an old, fat lady asked majestically.

I shook my head. "Sick boy," I said. "Please. Very, very sick boy . . . "

The airplane had lifted. We were in the air. The passengers protested loudly. I clamped him tight between my legs. He pushed his legs and arms against me furiously. A paper cup sailed through the air. "Take him to the bathroom. Take him to the bathroom . . . " cried the fat old lady loudly, shaking her finger at me. "There! Didn't I tell you? Sweet Jesus! Sweet Jesus!" And sure enough, a puddle had formed on the floor.

"Schatzi! Schatzi!"

I heard the drone of anger through a searing sheet of pain. A bald man shouted: "I've had it! I've had it! My daughter paid five hundred dollars for me to take this trip . . . " I tried to stand; I tried to lift my offspring by the armpits. "Please, Erwin. Please . . . " The fascinated passengers watched, entertained and terrified. The stewardess dispatched free drinks, and as she came near, Erwin hurled himself against her, a torpedo. Her tray flew into the aisle. I jumped to help her, to apologize, and found myself, astonished, on my knees. A searing pain had thrown me there. The bald man, cursing loudly, reached down to give me an impatient shove. I felt all color drain from my face as the pain, suspended for a moment, went razorsharp into my womb.

I was miscarrying.

It was a nightmare—that's all that I can say. Erwin leaped up and down in the aisle like a dervish possessed. He hooted. He squealed. He shrieked. He broke free and launched into a panicky run, heading blindly for the cockpit. Erwin carried fire in his head—he shook off hands and feet trying to restrain him. On spastic feet, he tried to sprint the length of the airplane. I knew that I was bleeding badly now—a fibrous fist pushed out of me. "Sweet Jesus. Sweet Jesus," moaned the fat lady, jumping up to make a grab. Erwin leaped like a fish in her arms. The bald man, incensed, decided to come to her aid—he grabbed Erwin's ear and gave it a mean little twist. That did it. All the passengers erupted. The stewardess knelt on his back, trying to wrestle him down. Voices hummed about me like a swarm of angry bees. I tried to stand, to help, but found that I could not, and so I sat, vilified and helpless, watching the ghoul I had borne writhe on the floor, fighting all hell's demons now, letting out scream after unearthly scream. I knew he could no longer recognize my voice, fired on by unremitting voltage deep within his injured brain. There I sat, ten thousand feet in the air, bound for eight hours of overseas flight, and wished that I would die.

"Hold him tight," the stewardess instructed me sternly. "Don't let him loose. And have a drink, OK?"

He lurched for my glass. "It's alcohol . . . " cried the girl, but had it been poison, would I have cared? He needed to drink a great deal after each of his fits to replenish the liquid he lost to his wild perspirations. He downed my gin-and-tonic with one gulp. His mouth stopped twitching at once. He looked at me, befogged. He turned pasty. The bald man shook a yellow finger. "He crazy?" he wanted to know. "He coocoo? He nuts?" My offspring went limp and slid to the floor.

"Please, bathroom . . . " I told the stewardess weakly. I followed her, staggering, wondering if I had managed to bleed through my coat. I bolted the door. I laid Erwin on the floor. I thought in a careening haze: "Just five or ten minutes . . . "

It took more than ten minutes. It took close to two hours to end another growing life. I sat, doubled over, my feet on Erwin's heaving body to keep him on the floor. The stewardess rattled the doorknob. I told her: "Please. Boy asleep. In a minute . . . " I sat, my head on the porcelain bowl, awash with blood and pain but strangely lightheaded.

This, too, had come to an end.

I could not tell if a baby had formed. I did not want to look. I pushed the lever and watched the bluish water swirl and swirl.

I washed myself as best I could. I cleaned up the bloody sink, the bloody toilet seat. I believe I even slept a little, with my head against the cold, scrubbed vanity.

When I thought that I could walk, I stepped over Erwin, now sound asleep on the floor. I made my way down the aisle, all the while fighting fog. The stewardess appeared and steadied me. She lifted Erwin from the floor. She put him next to me, across two empty seats, a little body limp at last, a hornet rendered helpless.

We landed in Zurich. A short cloudburst had muddied the streets. I took Erwin by the hand. He, pale and staggering, sporting a gigantic drug-and-alcohol hangover, stepped into every puddle.

I did not think that I could walk, but once I started, I managed. Luckily, a bus was waiting by the ramp. It took us to the train. The ride into the Black Forest took more than two hours. Customs officers peered at me through thick, worried glasses. Vas I alright? Vat vas ze matta?

I said I was a little ill.

Vy, she speaks German. They smiled at me, and I smiled back. I bled and bled and bled. I sat in my corner, amassing precious minutes. Erwin, still groggy, slumped opposite me.

"Freiburg im Breisgau!" called the conductor, rattling the door. I took my youngster by the hand. Could I make it down the steps, up the ramp, across the street, all the way to that row of blue taxis?

I could, and I did.

I stood on German soil for the first time in more than sixteen years. A cab pulled up beside me. I opened the back door and pushed Erwin in. He jumped on the seat, trying to throw himself out of the window. His shoes were caked with Switzerland mud. Cab-driver rudeness, I later found out, comes with the trade. He took a deep breath and started to curse, loudly and with angry gusto. When he had finished, I said, trying to spare him that I understood what he had wished on me: "Please, to a hotel."

"Please vat?" he yelled.

"I need a hotel."

"Vell, vat hotel?"

"Just any. Please."

"Dere's van right dere."

"I cannot walk that far."

"Dey don't valk in Amerikka?"

I paid him the equivalent of a day's pay for driving me across the street, for ruining his chances for the day, for he vudd haff to take his car to haff it cleaned! He carried my suitcase.

With a resolute thud, he set it in front of the lobby. "Dey valk in Germany!"

I managed to fill out the forms for my room, fighting all the while black hungry tongues that kept lapping at my brain. I paid for two days, depleting my purse. With a feeling of relief beyond compare, I followed the bellhop who pushed open a door to a sun-flooded room. I saw my soul's salvation there: an enormous, old-fashioned bathtub sitting on clawed feet, bolted solidly into the tiles of centuries, high-backed and steep—a readymade fortress. I said to Erwin: "Sorry. Sorry. Here you go." With his spasticity, no way could he climb out! I threw a blanket after him, two pillows. That took my very last morsel of strength. I closed the door on his howls and put my fists to my ears and crept deep into the quilts of Germany. I spent the rest of the day buried there, trembling and bleeding, but somehow knowing without doubt: I had managed to come far. I could go farther, surely, tomorrow.

CHAPTER FIFTEEN

Die Kinderklinik

THE NEXT DAY I CHECKED my son into the Freiburg *Kinderklinik,* where they would make him well. A nurse put striped pajamas on him. Another one lifted him matter-of-factly into a crib with high, solid bars. "Nothing can happen to him behind bars," I kept thinking, happily.

I briefly met the doctor who had invited me to come. I was astonished at his youth, but was I here to quibble? I stood in the draft of the hall, still shivering a little, and recounted my saga of woe. "An odyssey," he said comfortingly, and I loved him for his soft, kind voice.

Then I sat outside, alone, on a bench for a while. I tried to focus my thoughts on what day of the week, what month of the year it must be. Time was still a blurry thing, devoid of any meaning.

"What day is today?" I asked a passerby.

"The last day of May," said he, lifting his hat, an old-fashioned German.

May 31st. My sixth wedding anniversary.

I found the clinic coffee shop and bought the biggest pot of coffee I could order. For me there's nothing in the world to match the comfort of a steaming cup of coffee — and here I was drinking it, free of flailing arms and legs, free of shrieks and howls and horror. A vague peace stole into my heart. I sat by the window, sipping cup after cup, assessing the ways of the world and my as-yet-undefined place in it.

I must find work. At once.

The small cafeteria filled up, chair by chair. A young man asked to share my table. He told me that he had just moved to Freiburg, a pre-med student from up north. And who was I? He leaned forward eagerly. What was I doing here?

"I'm from Canada," I told him. "But during the war I lived near Hannover. It must have been—let's see—in 1945."

"That's the year I was born."

I told him: "I lived for many years in South America. As an adult, I came to Canada, and now I have returned, a woman almost thirty, to seek help in my homeland for my handicapped child."

"You speak German as they did two hundred years ago," he said smilingly, and I told him of the Russian-German Mennonites who had been part of me but who had cast me out. I talked and talked and talked. Gratitude, black German coffee, nostalgia, weakness, his deep friendly voice unleashed wordy torrents within me. He was clearly touched and flattered. I don't remember his name any more, but I clearly remember his face. It softened more and more with sympathy. "Work?" he said. "Why, that is the least of your worries." Could I wash dishes? Scrub floors? He had an aunt, a nun, in charge of Infectious Diseases. On that floor, they always needed help. Few people were willing to work in Infectious Diseases. The pay was a pittance, but room, board and full medical coverage were part of the package. Would I like to try?

I went back to my hotel. Yes, I could handle tomorrow after a day like today. I counted my money. Tossing caution to the wind, I put my thumb to the knob by the door.

"A full German dinner," I told the eager bellhop. "Everything that goes with it. *Sauerbraten, Rotkohl, Butterknoedel . . .*"

Oh, with what gusto I ate! Afterwards I ran a bath. I soaked in the fragrant waters with leisure. I felt as if this day had put a gentle dressing on a gaping, hideous wound. I stood released from my burden. And though I would yet have to learn to walk, my feet no longer were bound. A stillness came to me at last. I cherished my stillness, my tormentor gone. Three weeks, the doctor had said, would be needed to give me an answer. Three weeks translated to twenty-one nights. All to myself. Without interruption. Was there any deeper blessing in the world?

For twenty-one days, weekends included, I soaped the floors of sixteen rooms, three long halls, five bathrooms, three pantries, a staircase, and a kitchen the size of a mess hall. It was hard work, but I knew myself fully at peace. I did not tell a soul that only days ago I had miscarried. I felt as if this were some shameful, stupid thing that I had done. I must at all costs conceal it from anyone's knowledge.

For years, I felt like that about the things my body did to me.

And there were practical considerations, too. I feared that if I told, I would lose all: work, board and room, safety, insurance for Erwin, the heady feel of my first self-earned pay.

At each break, I would run to Erwin's ward.

He sat huddled in his crib. They had put him in a room with half a dozen other children who entertained themselves by taunting him. It helped them pass the time. They made faces at him and laughed at his upsets and fed him gobs of candy through the bars. Watching them tore at my heart. I am sure there was no malice in their actions. They were bored; he was a ready target. But, yes, it hurt to see him treated like an animal. But who was I to quibble now? He was safe. He was kept clean. He ate with a good appetite and, luckily, he did not seem to miss me much.

The doctors kept telling me that many tests were being run. Yes, they would rush. Soon, we would have a professional summary meeting. I would get full answers to all of my questions, *jawohl!*

With renewed vigor I would return to scrub my afternoon floors. A long dark descent had come to an end. My soul began to throw off its shackles.

After three weeks, I met with the medical team. I sat in a cool, immaculate office and listened carefully to what wise men and women had to say.

I guess I expected a ready-made plan, some kind of direction, a solid strategy that would lay it out for me: what I must do, where I must go, how I might educate Erwin. Nothing of the sort! When I left, I took more questions back than I had brought to Germany.

And yet, the meeting brought a circle to a close.

It was a solemn occasion, full of huge words that had little meaning, but also full of kindness and concern from unhurried doctors who spoke in my tongue. They spread their papers out. Here was the air encephalogram. Quite unremarkable. Here was the EKG. Perfectly normal. Here were the results of the chromosome tests. Nothing there, surprisingly. The EEG. Well within normal limits, with perhaps a mite of deepened Alpha waves. Amino acid studies. Normal. X-rays. Normal except for two large burr holes in his skull. Perhaps his wrists were slightly immature? And he seemed to be hypoglycemic. Did he crave sugar a lot?

I nodded to that. Yes, he was very fond of sweets.

It would behoove me to cut down on sugar.

I would.

"Has he ever had convulsions as a child?" Quite possibly there was residual epilepsy. I might want to give him Mysolin. A pill that would help to cut down on his rages.

" . . . a potent drug. May have some side effects and can be quite addictive. But given our limited options . . . "

" . . . combined with a restricted diet . . . "

" . . . and given the fact that he is getting older, more mature . . . "

It was a low-key, kindly session that seemed to offer much support. "But what about his future," I wanted to know. "What can he learn? What might he do? Where can I take him?"

"Your son scored an IQ of 50." This was my first encounter with a psychologist. "It means that, mentally, he will grow half as fast as normal children would . . . "

I stared at him. He said, after a long, painful pause: " . . . a seven- or eight-year-old can be quite bright, don't you agree . . . ?"

Yes, I did. I was grateful to the point of tears that a pill had been found, a diet had been recommended that would permit my child to grow exactly half as fast as normal children do.

I have often since remembered this meeting, the first of many such to come.

All that was said in Germany turned out to be quite true. In later years, Mysolin did make a difference, and so did a sugar-free diet, and so did maturation. And yet, today, as a psychologist myself, I know I was misled. It is not true that an IQ of 50 stands for " . . . half the intelligence a normal child would have." There is no way to measure "half" of what we call intelligence. In normative terms, an IQ of 50 is the pits.

It is so low that, if I were to go to any school and randomly select 100 children, probably not one would score as low as Erwin did. In terms of educational prognosis, an IQ of 50 is abysmal. A teacher in a conventional school will rarely encounter such a child. Textbooks may well have told that teacher: "A child like that will never know his family, will never know his way around the neighborhood, will never carry on a conversation, will never ever function normally." That's what the textbooks would have said.

But "IQ" meant nothing to me. I had never heard of such a designation. I did not know that IQs could be used, would be used in later years to bar my child from school. All I knew that day was this: three weeks ago I had come here with empty hands, and "half a life" seemed worth a try. "Half a life" seemed riches. And therefore I asked, reassured: "If he can function half as well as any normal youngster would, what about school? What about reading? Will he write? Will he add, subtract . . . " and, with my voice entangling itself on that burr in my throat: " . . . please, will he ever talk with meaning?"

The silence crept around the table. One of the lady doctors broke it finally. She said, her steady gaze on me: "Dear child, who is to say . . . ?"

CHAPTER SIXTEEN

My Child *Will* Read

I resolved: no more tears.

Woldi waited for us at the airport, more than willing to believe what I had decided we must now believe: it was only a matter of finding The School.

"Whatever it costs, we will manage," Woldi kept saying, hugging us both. I wondered just how we would manage. He never knew the balance of our bank account. I could not lean on him for solace and for strategies; he would forever lean on me. But he loved us in his own quiet, steady way—he would work hard and give us every penny and never once complain. I saw years of struggle before me. I quenched a small inner voice that wanted to know: " . . . just how many years?" I quenched it resolutely. I looked at him and wanted to know: Didn't he think the pills made a difference? Wasn't Erwin calmer to the touch?

"Oh, yes. I can see that," Woldi said agreeably and, whistling, drove us home.

There *was* a difference. Erwin's tension lessened visibly, once he was on medication and on a diet without sweets. He no longer spun in circles on the floor. He no longer chewed on coat sleeves. He no longer bit himself and others, drawing blood. We still faced old dilemmas: if a tooth broke in a comb, we must hide it, lest we make him shiver for three days. If there were a puddle somewhere, he would find it and step in. It was still wild laughter, sudden hives, days of choking nausea. If a word, a phrase stuck in his brain, he must repeat-repeat-repeat it. But there were glimpses now that made us hope.

We discovered, for example, that he had a built-in "inner clock" that functioned by strange, immutable rules. If we lived by its dictates, we could trade for a precarious peace. He was using it, by what means we could not fathom, to hold himself together tenuously. If he set his bedtime at exactly 8:04, it could not be at 8:06 or 8:08. It must be 8:04 precisely. We had to regiment our lives around that need, and it was difficult and frustrating, but it was simpler than seeing him shatter — a mind reduced to smithereens by the unbearable stress of just a few minutes' delay. It gave us a much-needed structure.

We came to understand: if he could grasp a solid time slot, we did not have to worry that a frightening or frustrating event would dement him — he need not dread having his world fall apart if a button were missing or the mailman were late. Set a mold and keep to it, and see him walk on fragile ice. Break his mold of expectation, and see him drown before your eyes. Time, to this day, is his most important intellectual skeleton and inner frame of reference. Yet it was many years before he could learn to "tell time" by conventional means.

I noticed something else: he had a sense of direction and location as acute as that of a bat. If he assumed — why, we did not know — that we would go to the Dominion Store, we could not then do violence to his inner map by going to the A&P. Given structure, given constancy, given order, he could hang on.

Yes, there was progress.

He would sit with us at breakfast now.

He could manage a night with no more than two or three modest nightmares.

I could let go of his arm. On good days I could lean back and catch my breath and look at him — without having to jump, without having to wrestle.

I observed: His brain functioned much like a camera or a tape recorder — nothing was ever lost in his head. All sounds, all impressions were stored and recorded. He saw everything. He heard everything. He could not sort and cut and edit.

Woldi cleared a space for a work bench in a corner of our basement, and there Erwin would behave at times as if he knew the rudiments of imaginary play. He would stack and re-stack pieces of lumber. He would gather piles of sawdust, flatten them, push them up again to rounded mounds. One day he picked up a hammer and managed to drive a straight nail. It fastened two pieces together. He looked at them ecstatically.

"Why, look! You fixed yourself an airplane!" I said, making it spin.

"You-fixed-yourself-an-airplane," he would tell me every morning, heading for the basement stairs.

The sentence had become attached to playing in the cellar.

Given this cue, he could not do something other than head for the stairs. He had no trouble forming words, though they were meaningless and repetitious and often paired with stimuli whose relevance became obscure. If a salesman happened to drop by, and chance would make me say: "I will be with you in just a few minutes . . . " just at the moment when a door hinge moved and his attention fastened on that door hinge, *any* hinge that moved could bring that sentence forth. He behaved as if he were "stuck" — as a needle gets stuck in the groove of a record. I tried to saturate this crazy, weird disorder. I would open and shut doors. Thirty times. Forty. The more I pressured him, the more he was compelled to spew forth his repetitious nonsense. It was easier for me not to open the doors of my cupboards. I also left my oven door alone until he could manage to shed his obsession with hinges.

Once he ran his hand over my knee in a strangely gentle gesture and asked: " . . . are-you-wearing-hose . . . ?"

"Why, *Schatzi,* yes . . . " I said, touched by what seemed to be meaning.

Was it my hug? My glad reply? The sensuous feel of fine synthetics on his fingers? For a span of some six months, he could not come near me without having to ask: " . . . are-you-wearing-hose . . . ?" I begged him to stop. I tried to ignore it. I said I would spank him. Driven to the edge, once or twice I did. He himself was torn the most. He would put his fists to his mouth. He would moan. He would whimper. With clenched teeth he would still have to ask, almost choking on his words the moment I appeared: "Are-you-wearing-hose?"

There is a name for it. It is called perseveration, a damaged mind's strange inability to stop an action once begun, the symptom of a mind at the mercy of some powerful but inappropriate learning. It dawned on me: it wasn't that he could not learn. He learned too well. He could not shake his learning, shrug it off. He went around, electrified for days by constant prodding irritants to nerve cells — " . . . are-you-wearing . . . " To an inordinate degree, Erwin suffered all through childhood from this weird affliction — a child hitched painfully to trivia.

If he could learn, I knew that I would find a way to build the rudiments of meaning. When he was three or four, I had once told him sharply: "Hot! No!" In time he came to understand my "No!" as "Hands off!" I forced myself never to use these two important cues in any other context. I didn't know it then, but I had hit upon the basic rule of behavioral psychology: if simple learning was to happen, it must be introduced and strengthened by rigid systems of reward. Reward and punishment are the all-purpose keys that open the door to complex behavior. Without precise rewards and punishments, all learning is hindered and blurred.

Once Erwin grasped these two small concepts, I tried to stress some higher rules: those of opposites, those of consequences, those of deduction. If it were night, it could not be day. If he dressed warmly, he would not be cold. If he could not find me in the kitchen, in all likelihood he would find me someplace else. He must then go and look for me—he must not sit and howl. If he looked for me, I would hug him for his ingenuity. If he howled—why, I would not. If he was "disobedient" within the rules that he could understand, he would be "punished," and if he followed these same simple rules, he would be greatly loved. It took a long time until he had grasped that doing things "right" meant rewards; doing things "wrong" meant rejection.

How I was censured by friend and foe alike for being so unyielding! How badly this rule is still disobeyed with limited children today. "Just love 'em," misguided saints will spread their exhortations, "and miracles are bound to follow." Not so. We don't build satellites with "love." We don't need "love" to conquer space. We don't presume we have to "love" abundantly when we teach swimming or baseball or chess. We pair skill and know-how and precision with specific strategies. I believe that we have opened doors to a barbaric misconception when it comes to a handicapped child: that love will conquer all. It can't. How dare we say that if we only love enough we can heal wounds that are of an organic nature? How dare we think that love alone will do it for a bludgeoned mind? It is impossible. There has to be discrimination of response. The sooner we adhere to evolutionary principles of learning, the better off our limited children will be.

I held that knowledge, tenuously, when I took both children by the hand to start their formal schooling. Rudy was soon-to-be five, just old enough to register. Erwin was six, almost seven. He should have started school the previous year, but I had taken him to Germany and he had missed the registration date. It did not matter then; I knew he could not have coped. But now a year had passed. He had calmed down a lot. I felt that, as a start, I should give public school a try.

I might as well have known. Within the hour I was summoned. I was to pick him up! and take him home!! and keep him there!!! till further official notice. The teacher, a very young girl, kept swallowing tears. Rudy clung to me, sobbing in wretched confusion. Erwin huddled in a corner, a hellcat on the loose.

In early afternoon, there was a sharp knock on my door. The St. Catherine's school superintendent, flanked by two specialists, sat down in my living room. Stiffly. I served coffee. They served ultimatums. He was different, special — right? I could see that — could I not? He had needs unlike those of normal children? I was smart — I would agree. They could tell, just looking at me, that I was smart and sensible.

I said: "Yes, I agree. Where can I take him so he can learn to read?"

"Well . . . " said one.

"Ahem . . . " said the other.

"Well . . . ahem . . . " said the third. There was a special place. With lots of loving teachers. A very, very special school.

"It's called Rosegarden School," said one.

"Ah, yes," sighed the other. "a wonderful, wonderful school. With wonderful, wonderful teachers."

"He will be so happy there," the superintendent assured me, and the two specialists nodded, beaming at me.

Would I sign a document to that effect? That I agreed he would not benefit from regular instruction?

I said: "I have been told that he can learn to read."

"Well . . . " said one.

"Ahem . . . " said the other.

"Well . . . Ahem . . . " said the third.

At that time, I knew next to nothing about the politics of public schools, about my rights, my child's right to an education. I only knew: in Germany I had been promised half a life, and nothing short of half a life would do.

"Please sign here," said one.

"On the dotted line," said the other.

"Yes, please do," said the third. "It would save us much trouble. For sure."

I see them still. They sat there in my living room, nodding to each other wisely. Such wonderful, wonderful teachers. A wonderful, wonderful school.

Nothing, nothing prepared me!

I know today: what I was made to see at Rosegarden that day could not have been the worst. I have since been to many institutions, many schools. As a matter of fact, it might well have been one of the better schools for the "trainable retarded." It was clean. Airy. Well-scrubbed. It faintly smelled of bleach and urine, as all these places do. There were displays of frilly hearts and valentines, grinning paper suns and peevish moons, elephants and Easter bunnies, paper chains and fat balloons.

Nowhere could I see a blackboard.

Nowhere did I see a book.

What I saw was horror upon horror. I had never encountered, up close, another profoundly damaged small child, much less so many of them almost grown: with tongues hanging out of mouths that gaped at me, with crooked hands that clawed at me, with eyes that bulged and skin that blistered and voices that grated and grunted and bleated and bayed.

There is no way to say it gently: to me, it was Dante's Inferno, and I had not known.

Every cell in my body recoiled. My child was different — surely! Even now, I struggle for comparisons that will explain just what I saw and felt that day. Here is the truth, plain and simple, and you may stone me for it if you like: It was like encountering maggots — fat and slow and mindless and repulsive beyond words. What I was made to see that morning, unprepared, I cannot forget for as long as I live. Not in my worst nightmares had I ever seen anything like it. I kept struggling for air. Was this what Erwin would be like in just a few more years?

"Lambs on God's merciful bosom," gushed the lady who showed me around. How precious they were, these droll, hapless things. Each and every one of them, in time, would wear a diamond crown. With prayers and love we must hoist them in the meantime. With the patience of Job.

I swallowed many times, and when I could, I asked: "What about reading . . . ?"

She snapped sharply to attention. It was as if she saw a serpent rear its head.

"These children," she said primly, "Do. Not. Read."

I said: "I have been told my child will learn to read."

"He won't," she said. "Mark my word. None of them do. Never. You might as well face that right now."

I said: "My child will read."

"Well, yes," she said, suffering greatly. "Just push him. And push him and push him. And see where *that* will get you in the end."

To her defense, and mine, let it be said: She was of German stock, and therefore loathe to mince her words. But so, dear Lord, was I. And she and I were Mennonites—in the hall we had discovered that to our mutual dismay. She was the better one, it now turned out—for she was born in Canada, while I was just a recent immigrant, no doubt expecting life on a silver platter. She knew about unrealistic expectations held by immigrants. What was wrong with this fine school? This was a wonderful, wonderful school. With wonderful, wonderful teachers.

I have forgotten her name. It no longer matters. But in those days, a glance could rip open old wounds, and she had fistfuls of salt for the asking: wasn't I the one who had packed up and gone to Germany, spurning good Canadian doctors? Who never went to Sunday services—not once in some four years? Who broke her husband's mother's heart? It was her holy duty to suggest I take my cross and search my heart and crawl back to the bosom of my people.

I said again: "My child will read." I sat in her office, declaring open war.

"Go ahead," she said, viciously. "Go right ahead. You'll learn. I mean, after all. What choices do you have? Really!"

I said I had the choice to fight.

"You'll end up here," she said. "You'll see. I know it."

Blast her to the darkest spot in a pitch-black unforgiving universe! I cried: "Rosegarden? Never. Never. Never. I'll leave. I'll move."

"Ah, yes," said she, a righteous sufferer who must put up with fools. "To the end of the world you will move. Go right ahead and move. Go right ahead and ruin yourself. And your health. And your marriage. And your family. You'll still be back. You'll still end up here. At Rosegarden. Or at a place just like it. Mark my word."

Prophetic words indeed. How often have I since remembered them. Was she right? Or was she wrong? Today, the countless battles for the academic rights of my hurt child are milestones in public school law. Dearest lady, he did learn to read and write. He has finished public high school — with academic honors. He holds a job. He pays his share of taxes, just as you and I. He tells me in his latest letter that he is going to Hawaii on a pre-paid ticket bought with money he has saved. He tells me that he dates a lovely girl named Teri. He asks me how I am, he tells me not to work so hard, he worries if my headaches plague me still, he tells me he is proud of me, he tells me that he loves me. Once or twice each week, I receive a long missive.

Would that have been possible, had I given in? Never. I know that. But there are two sides to every heartache coin. He now lives at the Good Shepherd Home. It serves the mentally retarded.

CHAPTER SEVENTEEN

The Academy

I drove home that day, knowing myself irreversibly altered. Psalms and prayers and no pencils? Love and pity and no books? Good intentions without know-how? No. And no. And no.

For years afterwards, "God's will" translated to a blotchy face set hard against me with a hollow, rigid hatred. This mealy-mouthed zealot, no doubt with all the best intentions in the world, made me as sick and mad and violent as anything that life had thrown my way so far. Not my little finger's nail would I render to such a sick rendition of "God's will." Let the righteous, let the faithful keep their Rosegardens to have a place to shine their lights. I would proudly walk in darkness. Any day and any time.

At home, I found a letter in my mail box. The schools of St. Catherine's were willing to help. As a matter of fact, the schools of St. Catherine's were eager to help. A niche for every child—that was their written policy. Would I give my consent for some testing?

That puzzled me. I had already given them the test results from Germany. Did this mean that there were other choices? There was the dotted line, again. For me to sign. Was it my fate to ponder dotted lines?

I duly pondered.

Then I signed.

What could be worse than Rosegarden?

This was a time when IQs were writ large. Erwin's IQ, as measured in German, was truly abysmal. As measured in English, he had no IQ. That was no surprise to me, for I sat in and listened to the questions. My English was still woefully inadequate; I did not understand a fourth of what the toothy testing lady said. How could Erwin understand the questions in a foreign tongue when I spoke to him in German, when he hardly spoke at all?

The very next day I was curtly informed that, on the basis of scientific evidence, Erwin did not qualify for any kind of help in public schools, and that, regrettably, was that.

I had seen it coming, but still it was a shock. A little number did it. Neatly. No trial. No testimony. No lawyers. No probationary period. The lowliest criminal in Canada had better recourse to a public education than had a little boy.

I came to hate IQs and learned to fight them savagely. Others had done it before me. Others have done it since. I found them that spring, those "others." They called themselves the ACLD — the Association for Children with Learning Disabilities.

"Learning disabilities are specific disabilities," this combative group proclaimed. "They range from mild to most severe. They should not be confused with mental retardation. Potentially, learning-disabled children have normal or even superior IQs. They suffer from a circumscribed disorder . . . " A mongoloid, or so it was explained, had every single body cell "unfinished," while our children had their imperfections localized — presumably a lot of good cells and some bad.

The point was: they were different.

The message: teach the good cells. The good cells can be taught.

Sweeter words were never heard. This was a group of parents struggling just as hard as I was, speaking in behalf of what came to be known as the "perceptually handicapped" or "minimally brain-damaged" child. We shortened that in time to MBD. The terminology, the wild and unsubstantiated claims would bother me a little. While I had to quarrel with the former designation, in my heart I felt: the latter did not fit. Erwin's damage was not "minimal." While I knew that it was localized, I also knew that it was massive. I knew it all too well.

But still. They seemed to say what I had not the means or words to say. They wrapped their rhetoric around my own inarticulation, and so I paid my dues and joined them formally and sat fervently through many a volatile meeting. I added my time, my presence, my pennies, my name to their goals: Better identification. Intelligent public awareness of the plight of the mind-injured child. Well-trained teachers. Special budgets. Separate classes. A tailor-made curriculum. No dumping grounds. No Rosegardens for our boys and girls. Let that be clearly known.

I sat and listened and learned some very useful slogans, feeling other parents' hurts and disappointments fuel my own. No longer did I need to feel so helplessly, so totally alone. By Heaven, I was not the only one wounded!

What a heady, glorious, militant time! We marched upon school board meetings *en masse:* " . . . we have children who can learn if you have teachers who can learn to teach them." We made sure a sympathetic press was there. We rang up universities: "What? You haven't yet heard of a perceptual-motor deficit? And you are training future teachers? How backwards can you be . . . ?" We called entrenched psychologists: "You say you have no test? Hocus pocus—here's a test. For auditory memory. For receptive and expressive visual discrimination. And here, if you please, is one that measures auditory closure. This one's for figure-ground disturbances. And here's a screening instrument for integrative therapy . . . " We badgered local papers: " . . . ten million citizens suffer from a perceptual disorder. Fifteen percent of all school age children are in need of some kind of specialized help . . . "

We rode clouds of fire in those days. We had more momentum than direction, but we set in motion some enormous legislative gears. It took us many years, but how we fought, and how we lobbied! We made handsome gains in the generous Sixties. Watch your bandwagon — just hop aboard. Teacher, are you stifled with your present job? Why, with just a little summer training, you can become a Learning Specialist. How about a master's thesis in disturbances in tactile, visual, and auditory learning? Here's a list — ask for a grant. We called our representatives: " . . . you haven't heard of Billy who is smart but cannot learn? Why, just yesterday, the local paper ran a story. Use your Xerox. Spread the word. Put your weight behind our cause, or we won't put our vote behind your name . . . "

Wild claims and promises were cheap. A great deal of nonsense was hatched. We see it all too painfully today in public schools. But that is a different story.

But in those days, we all agreed. There simply was no choice. And so we kept on pushing hard, in many different directions. We had a name that lacked precision, we stood on shifting shores pedagogically and diagnostically, but we were ready to eat fire, swallow swords. There were dumping grounds all over Canada and the United States called Rosegardens, and our children were not going there.

Even then, in the midst of all this warring on behalf of a just cause, I felt vaguely disturbed. For we claimed, repeatedly: " . . . the disability may be so mild you wouldn't know you had it, or so severe that it might cripple every aspect of your life." That was a very wide umbrella. Just about any critter could hide underneath. I felt that, in our eagerness, we built defeat into our gains. We had set out to help a very special child — the brain-injured child, the mind-damaged child. Not the dullard. Not the disturbed. Not the deprived. Not the delinquent. Not the socially maladjusted. And by golly — not the mistaught!

In my opinion, much harm need not have happened, had we kept better watch on our definitions from the start. In the end, we midwifed a farce in our eagerness for sharp and appropriate labels. We struggled for labels—we wanted them, we needed them, we felt that any kind of diagnostic label would buy us better teachers, smaller classes, better funding for our schools.

For here's the irony and paradox: Schools today get paid for labelling. Handsomely. Publishers sell useless programs based on labels we dreamed up in our eagerness and haste. The testing industry continues to spew tests that are of very little value. As all teachers know, and as parents came to know in time, a label does not guarantee appropriate treatment. Much less a "cure." A label does not even target therapy.

A label is only a label. To box children in.

All this I say in retrospect, now sitting on the other side, under public pressure daily as a certificated "labeller" to label poor teaching, poor parenting, laziness, lack of motivation, lack of sleep or lack of vitamins or just plain clumsy feet " . . . an MBD disorder" or " . . . a perceptual deficit."

But I am a decade ahead of myself.

When I first joined the ACLD, my needs and aims were simple. I needed a label, for I was in search of The School. The ACLD was quick to provide me with both—long lists of schools, and long and ornamental lists of labels. I was astonished to find out how many schools did actually exist that made use of these fanciful labels. Big and small. Prominent and obscure. Open and hidden. Half day schools. Full day schools. Year-round schools. Camps for special children. Schools for the non-ambulatory. For the multiple handicapped. For the mentally disturbed.

I could not help noticing: The costlier the schools, the more euphemistic the label. And the higher the tuition, the lesser weight was given to IQs. How could that be? Given money, given means, could IQs just "disappear"—be stricken from a youngster's records? I brooded a great deal over this seeming puzzle, but it took me many years until I truly understood the underlying economic fact: a cruel, shameless money racket was feeding off IQs — that is, parents' desperate need to deny them, to avoid having to deal with the label "retarded." Parents were willing to pay through the nose for not having to say: "My child attends a school for the retarded." For a price in the thousands of dollars, parents could rightfully claim:

"My child attends a special language school . . . "

"My son is going to a therapeutic summer camp . . . "

"My daughter is involved in music therapy . . . "

All the "better" schools closed doors on me after studying the "evidence" — that is, the dual handicap of "no IQ" and inability to pay. Erwin was seven now, going on eight. No, he had never been to school. Yes, he was toilet-trained, but, no, he could not speak, not yet. But he was forming words that seemed to have some meaning, and although we could not pay the full tuition and would need help, but only temporarily, we were more than willing . . .

Slam! went the door.

Sorry.

I have changed some names in the following passages to write about the not-so-innocent. I don't know how else to tell this story.

I'll call it The Academy. It advertised itself as a school for " . . . speech and related disorders." It was a private boarding school, and I found it through a friend. It had a residential campus, featured prominently on the cover of a glossy brochure that came in the mail — spacious, fenced in brick, inviting. All its scholastic features, as described in detail, seemed so tailor-made, so perfect for our needs that I could not believe I had in the past overlooked it. It was legitimate all right: university-affiliated, offering a " . . . comprehensive program to serve all the needs of the speech-impaired child." It was located in the very heart of North America. And here I could read, in response to my query, that this world-renowned school was willing to give us a try.

No IQs.

No restrictions as to age, ability, degree of damage, color, race, or sex.

No questions whatsoever asked.

I searched for the flaw. Tuition was high, to be sure. If we added room and board, the amount roughly equaled our income. But here it said, in black and white, right underneath the picture of a smiling, pigtailed youngster: "Many children are helped to reach full potential thanks to generous sponsorship aid . . . "

I wrote and requested a visit. I was granted a visit posthaste.

We emptied our savings account. Erwin and I boarded a train. Once we arrived at our destination, I watched all kinds of friendly, smiling people run him through all kinds of tests. At four o'clock sharp, they assembled. Yes, they all agreed with me: what a shame—the little fella here had never been to school? High time indeed to get him going.

Costs? It kept nagging me. I wanted to know.

Well, they were high. A smiling gentleman, who shall be known as Mr. Thompson, wanted to know: How much could we pay?

Not much. The testing and the trip alone had just about exhausted my resources.

"No problem. No problem," Mr. Thompson assured me. Would we consider moving perhaps? If Erwin could reside with us, that would reduce the bill substantially by eliminating costly room and board. Would I write to Immigration? Get a feel for the red tape involved? Meanwhile, Mr. Thompson kindly offered to place Erwin's name on the Baton Twirlers' list.

Mr. Thompson kept stressing this list. Although I could not understand at first, I came to grasp it as a world-wide philanthropic enterprise.

Mr. Thompson tapped his desk and smiled and smiled and smiled. "Many children are on scholarships from private organizations, such as the Baton Twirlers. Or helped by local, state, or federal aid." No child, stressed Mr. Thompson, was ever turned away for lack of funds. Would I agree to place Erwin's name on The List?

Would I?!

So funds in his behalf could be solicited?

Of course!!

It might take a while until he could actually start. Mr. Thompson wanted to be very sure I knew that.

Oh, yes. I understood. I would wait. Of course. Oh, gladly.

The List was long, stressed Mr. Thompson. He wanted to make sure I understood that The List was very long.

I said: "I will stand in line."

"All right then," said Mr. Thompson briskly. "First things first. Let's get a folder started. Why don't you go home and relax? And keep in touch? And write a little note to Immigration . . . ?"

I sat there, giddy with relief, holding Erwin wedged between my knees. Where was the catch? There seemed to be none. Miraculously and incomprehensibly, I had found the Perfect School. And not a thing for me to do but wait.

We flew home that evening. I told Woldi, jubilant, that as soon as Erwin's name moved up the Baton Twirlers' list, all our problems would be solved.

U.S.A.

CHAPTER EIGHTEEN

The Midwest

BUT THEN SOMETHING VERY strange happened—or, more precisely, did not happen: nobody called us back. The strategy, as agreed upon by me and Mr. Thompson, had been that we would send Erwin " . . . as a child in need of therapy" ahead of us on a temporary visa, and our family would follow just as soon as our home was sold and our immigration papers cleared.

There seemed to be a snag with the Baton Twirlers' list.

By mistake, another child—or so it seemed, from the vague, apologetic letter I received—had been taken on, and Erwin's name had dropped to the bottom.

We gritted our teeth and waited some more.

No progress. Days and weeks and months went by.

Erwin's suitcase stood packed, but he outgrew the pajamas inside. I wrote several times. I parked myself next to the mailbox. I called. Yes, he was still on the list. It was just a matter of waiting. Could I try to be a little patient? Everything was still in order—all systems set to go.

We waited for almost a year. Nothing seemed to move. Rudy, almost two years younger, was about to enter second grade. Erwin spent his days pulling thread out of my couch.

In the end we could no longer stand it. We rammed a "For

Sale" sign in front of our house, found temporary renters, and left for the United States to find out for ourselves.

Distance upon distance!

As our car gulped the turnpike in a hammering rain, I reveled in the feel of leaving all behind — sleepless nights, irritating phone calls, dreams unfulfilled and joys unknown. As we rolled through the Midwestern hills, the afternoon turned crisp and clear. Billowing clouds floated into the distance, and the sky became dotted with airplanes. There is a special feel to the Midwest in the wake of hefty, unexpected rain — one's very blood, it seems, deepens to a richer, fuller hue. Before us lay a brand new life. At long last the waiting was over.

"Look, there is The Academy . . . "

Triumphantly, we turned into the tree-lined U-shaped entrance. We checked in with Mr. Thompson, who seemed surprised and quite taken aback at seeing us on his doorstep quite so soon.

For a nominal fee and a small deposit, he informed us, recovering fast, we could rent a small apartment on the grounds. Living close would speed enrollment.

We signed up for three small, darkish rooms, a kitchen, and a bath with plugged-up plumbing. It turned out that our neighbor to the left was Mrs. Hall, a helpful, gentle lady, the widow of the founder of the school. She stood by her door and welcomed us warmly. "The place is full of bugs," said Mrs. Hall, apologetically. "Before you move your stuff in, you better use some *Raid*."

"I'll live in a snake pit," I told her while she helped me sweep the spiders from the windows. "As long as my son learns to read . . . "

"We have cockroaches, too," said Mrs. Hall mournfully. "This place was clean until my husband died . . . "

In sympathy, I listened to her tale. She was a disillusioned, grieving woman, her voice no longer wanted in the place her husband built and led for many years.

"Nobody seems to be in charge," she told me bitterly. "All programs are in disarray." Personality clashes. Disagreements as to leadership. A greedy institutional philosophy. No serious research. A jealous staff. Low morale among the old-time loyal workers. She sat in my kitchen, numb with her own penned-up pain.

Fear ate into me with sharp teeth.

Surely, this was a legitimate school? It had to be — it was a huge and sprawling complex that must have cost hundreds of thousands of dollars to build. It had affiliations with a university. With my own eyes I had seen the remarkable language department.

"How many children are served?" I wanted to know.

Mrs. Hall wasn't sure. "While my husband still lived, we served about two to three hundred . . . " But now? You never knew, what with those secretive administration policies.

I went to look around. It was a school all right — although there seemed to be more offices than classrooms. To the right lay the speech therapy rooms and, it seemed to me, three or four classrooms at best. Well, not classrooms, exactly — they looked more like sparsely furnished waiting rooms, with just a few tables and chairs. Some shabby toys were piled up in a corner. I saw a group of children huddle, loosely supervised by a young and sullen girl. An aide? An intermittent sitter? She just sat there, doing nothing. It was odd.

The rest of the "classrooms" were housed in the basement, and a few, a chain-smoking lady explained, pointing with a broken fingernail, " . . . spill over to the cottages located in the back." The halls of the basement were narrow. Wheelchairs cramped them even more. The air circulation was poor.

"How many children . . . ?" I wanted to know.

"Close to five hundred," she told me and shrugged.

It was strange. I could not shake an unsettling feeling. Where was the evidence of regular instruction? There were a few blackboards — I noticed them at once. And, yes, the children learned their ABCs, the lady said, lighting yet another cigarette, pointing to the stenciled letters on the walls. I peered into one of the rooms that resembled a regular classroom. On the table lay some colored pencils, newspaper clippings, perhaps a dozen cans containing dried-out paint next to a wet and frazzled, none-too-appetizing rag. By the door of yet another room hung some addition and subtraction charts. I saw some arts and crafts rooms, some pottery facilities, a music room, a physical therapy room. I peered into a smoke-filled cafeteria.

"It's summer," said my guide. "It looks a little desolate."

"How many children did you say?"

"Why, close to five hundred . . . "

Where could they be housed? I had seen a bus or two unload a handful of children, and some private cars pulled up beside the ramp and unloaded a few more. No playground outside. No bell. No regular recess. A few swings hung limp and deserted—Rudy mounted one and started swinging listlessly. In the late afternoon, there was a moderate commotion. A few children limped away. A few wheelchairs disappeared into the cottages—silent foster mothers pushing very silent youngsters. I struck up a clumsy conversation with one or two of the ladies. Just what did they do for their charges to help them learn to read? Blank stares. They had never considered that question.

Woldi found work as a welder and fitter. I throttled my mounting unease while awaiting admission of my child.

A week passed.

Two.

Three.

Once or twice, I waylaid Mr. Thompson: When could my son start school?

He said he would consult his records.

Mrs. Hall, sharing her washer and dryer and all her embittered opinions with me, said sharply: "Were my husband still alive, this would surely not have happened. What *are* they waiting for? If I were you, I would investigate."

Once again, I went in search of Mr. Thompson. I apologized for my unseemly impatience, but did he remember The List? A summer was just about gone.

"A few minor details," he assured me. Meanwhile, would I go and have some routine testing done? Check my family for allergies? Campus regulations.

Why, of course.

All four of us were poked and pricked and checked for an array of allergies.

Day after day went down the drain. Erwin was eight now, going on nine. Never for a single day had he attended classes. The summer days melted away as we waited to see him move up on The List.

I knocked on Mr. Thompson's office door and asked to be shown the mysterious list. I had now waited for more than a year. I was not going to wait any longer. I simply needed certainty.

A reddish sheen appeared on Mr. Thompson's neck. "Now, now . . . " he said. "Just what's the rush? Wait just a little minute . . . " He kept on shuffling through a stack of papers. I inched a little closer to have a peek myself. I said: "Mr. Thompson, tell me. Does such a list exist?"

"Goodness! Goodness gracious! Here—here it is! Your son was scheduled to start weeks ago! How could I have overlooked it? I am so sorry. Truly I am. Let me apologize. This job drives me batty. All these details . . . "

I said it again: *"Is* there a list?"

"Yes, here it is. Here it is! What's-his-name—Irving can start right away. It says so right here. You were right all along—how about that? I was wrong. Well, how about that? Bring him to the front reception room. At eight o'clock tomorrow morning. Sharp!"

I scrubbed him until he was pink. I slicked his hair and

brushed his teeth and dressed him in his finest sailor suit. A mindless nitwit? Not any more—not for much longer, anyway! Let him talk gibberish—for now. Let chaos march within his head—today. Tomorrow would be different, just given the tiniest chance. I kissed him over and over, giddy with the knowledge that the end—nay, the beginning—was near.

I took him by the hand and said: "Please, *Schatzi*. Try!" His fingers felt like putty.

A nice lady met us, all sunshine and smiles. She patted my hand. She took Erwin by the wrist. Together, the two disappeared.

Oh, for the mind-shattering silence that followed!

For the first time in almost a decade—discounting my brief interlude in Germany—I had six hours to myself to do as I pleased. I could go shopping. Or read. Or knit. Or visit with my neighbors. Or just sit in my chair, not moving the joint of my left little finger. And no one would come and scratch up my legs or writhe in my lap or chew on my shoes.

Did I have that cup of coffee I deserved?
No.

I had seen the scribbled notice by the door: "Typist Wanted." Why, with Erwin now enrolled, I could work to help defray the costs of schooling. I had helped a missionary once, eons back in Paraguay, and I had learned the rudiments of typing from an old instruction book. I resolved to brush up on my skills. If Erwin could indeed remain at school—oh glory! glory! glory! at the thought—I would gladly shoulder my share of the still murky matter of very expensive tuition.

The job turned out to be a cinch: Could I type two or three words, over and over and over? Dear Mr. Jones. Dear Mrs. Smith. Dear Dr. Hanson. Assembly-line fashion. Four hundred times per hour, eight hours per day, five days per week.

"Slightly monotonous work," explained the lady who interviewed me. She did not want to hire me if I had any doubts. It took a very special person to hang in there and type all day and really stick it out.

Dear Mrs. Simpson. Dear Mr. Hogan. Dear Dr. Fry.

Eight other girls hunched over their typewriters, silently pecking away. Dear Mrs. Brown. Dear Dr. Schneider. Dear Mrs. Watkins. Dear Mr. Jones.

We lifted names from coded lists. We worked from telephone directories. Certain people were approached via *pica,* while others were addressed in elegant *elite.* Some received a missive typed with a costly carbon ribbon. Others learned of Jesus' love in exchange for their donation via plain and somewhat smudgy spools. We fortified certain mailing lists with a proven contribution record with stamped, self-addressed envelopes, while others, yielding less, were designated one-way, coach. Some donors were promised rewards in the hereafter. Others were urged to save on their taxes, still others because civic pride was at stake.

Dear Mrs. Jones. Dear Mr. King.

Here was one, in the form of a flyer, featuring an excerpt from a parent: "I know that God must have wanted me to . . . " My heart rebelled at the simpering plea. If nothing else, the darkness that had settled on my life had brought a silent, stubborn dignity. This much I had sorted out for myself: there were limits to omnipotence as far as I could see.

Dear Mr. Trott. Dear Dr. Kessler. Dear Friend in Tennessee.

Somewhere along the way I had relinquished comfort emanating from a higher power. I could no longer claim, not even in the abstract, that He could heal a broken mind if only I would humble my hot and rebellious and obstinate heart. My heartbreak was meant to teach me a lesson? What lesson? How unfair. How obscene.

Dear Father Jones. Dear Mrs. Hollerman.

Just why? Just why?

Dear Friends of the Afflicted.

Just where was the lesson?

Dear Mr. Lowry.

Dear Mrs. Cook.

My fingers raced. My eyes blurred with the onslaught of humiliation and despair. Why must I beg like that? Was not my child entitled to a school, to an education, like any other child in America? What had he ever done to be cast out?

Dear Mrs. Higgins.

Dear Mr. Watts.

Stacks of paper to my left, upside down, rolled into my typewriter with a skilled little twist while I kept on wrestling with the demons. Ten fingers on ten keys. Left thumb and forefinger pulling out plea after plea, flipping it over, sending it across the cluttered desk. My giggly counter-typist caught them, folded them, flip-flop, sent them, flip-flop, to the girl-who-stuffed-the-envelopes. The girl-who-told-the-same-joke every day was a whiz at sealing letters. Swoooop! went the sponge, counter-clockwise, and sssshhht! went the stack, to be postage-stamped by the girl-who-smelled-of-garlic to the girl-who-double-checked: twenty, thirty at a time, a flung-out fan, flipped clear across the edge, sponge over rims. Bundle upon bundle of my pleas, neatly sorted as to zip codes, plummeted into the burlap bags that rolled along the grimy walls, bags pregnant with humiliation: " . . . won't you please spare me a couple of minutes to read about a little boy in need of your generous help . . . ?"

I took pencil and paper and figured it out. Two lifetimes of typing would not be enough to repay what it would cost. I was earning $150.00, subtract an array of deductions, per month. Tuition, books, and incidentals added up to almost twice as much.

I sat in the restroom, struggling with panic. When I came back, the foreman lady, having eyed me for a while, rose from her elevated chair to take me by the arm. "Take a break, hon', take a break," she said kindly, and put me in charge of sorting the loot coming in through the opposite door. Check after check tumbled out of coded envelopes. Now and then I unfolded a hand-written letter: "I know I am blessed, for my children are healthy in body and mind. Therefore, please accept . . . " Ten dollars. Twenty. A check for a fat round one-hundred. Why, look at that! Aaaahs and ohhhhs. A money order from Hawaii!

Dear Mrs. Hewett.

Dear Dr. Frost.

"Have a piece of cake," said the garlic-girl, giggling. "And watch it—don't get crumbs all over Kansas City." Hooting mirth. We always celebrated someone's birthday—we were a very jolly crowd. Did you hear the joke about the Avon Lady? Or the one about the chicken that refused to lay an egg?

At lunch, I ran across the parking lot to our apartment. My head was an aching balloon. I closed all doors and windows, locking silence in. It was mine, this precious silence. It must not escape, this wonderful thing. For forty-five minutes, nobody could claim it, destroy it, take it from me.

I moved as if under compulsion. I went after the mind-shattering silence. I followed it deeper and deeper—straight into the bathroom, locking it in. I fell right into it, onto my knees. Within that silence, a stranger started to whimper. The part of me that stood detached could hear the stranger whimper. Then sob. Then cry out. Then shriek. About this, about that, about the hideous pain that kept on gnawing nerve ends, about the waste of years that might have been, about the vicious odds against an anguished child who never knew a moment's peace and never would, about the many horrors that were yesterday and the ones that would be there again tomorrow, about the darts of guilt at night, about the treachery of love. I was a puppet on a string, and something had me by the throttle, commanding me to scream and scream and scream until this thing within me lost its voice, until it finally was satisfied and silenced and abandoned.

I realized I had not cried for years.

I lay, spent but at peace, my head on the lid of the bowl. I was covered, head to toe, with perspiration. Now I knew, first hand, the terrors of derangement. An autumn day still flashed outside. I had used up twelve minutes of my break. A wheelchair squeaked on the sidewalk. I stood on shaky knees, full of a fragile wonder. My feet had touched an abyss, but I had struggled free, I was still sane, I could still breathe, I lived!

I made myself over in front of a mirror. I even used lipstick that day.

CHAPTER NINETEEN

Surviving

AGE CAN BE MEASURED in many dimensions. My passport stated that I was thirty-one. I was Methuselah when measured by my struggles. But on that golden autumn afternoon in 1967, I turned brand-new, I stood reborn. Not to the Lord. Not to atonement. Not to reparations for my sins or restitution for my faults, and not to the dubious hope of a better hereafter. Not to a humbled, diminished existence in keeping with the darkness that my sin had settled on my child — I stood reborn to claim my intellect.

I know this without any doubt. I know it with that lucid clarity that only birth and death bestow. Had I not changed my direction, my spiritual scourge would in the end have finished me. Let it be said with deep inner pride that I, illiterate and all but destroyed, came to realize one simple, overwhelming truth: that as a Mennonite, I was miscast. It was that simple — I was miscast. And from that simple knowledge, once discovered, it was possible to choose with certain instinct the only road open to me: to claim that fruit plucked from the Tree of Knowledge that circumstances and upbringing had managed to withhold from me.

That crucial afternoon, I was nothing more than a blob of incoherent pain on some dingy, peeling tiles. When my convulsions receded, I realized this: I must have understanding. I must do something for myself—exclusively. I must secure some intellectual grasp about the nature of this hideous punishment that had fallen on my life, that had devoured half of it already. I must, come what may, recapture my claim to my own independent existence. I must weave for myself some measure of spiritual meaning or die.

Had I known of a psychiatrist, I would no doubt have knocked on his door. But I had never heard of Freud—or, for that matter, Doris Day, Twiggy, the Beatles. I had never dropped a coin in a pay telephone. I had never tried a K-Mart counter for a sandwich or a Coke. No beauty parlor operator had ever touched my hair. For seven long tormented years, I had lived "in the world," yet lived in a virtual prison—a prison from within and from without.

That afternoon, I held raw instinct for survival, and no more, in the hollow of my shaking hands.

Not far from The Academy's campus, sprawling on a hill of sorts, lay a university. Once or twice, I had been driven by. I knew it was a place of higher education—that was all I knew, that day. Naively, I visualized it passing out knowledge like soup in a ladle—the good ones, the worthy, were fed. With longing and envy I had observed astounding creatures stroll about its sidewalks—girls with long hair and short skirts, boys who sprawled on lawns and scattered books and talked in soft and languid tones and flirted with the girls. That day my hunger drove me there. I am convinced that, even as I went, I only hungered for proximity to knowledge. I just wanted to look. I just wanted to dream—just a little.

Behind those dark brick walls, I knew, lay worlds of brilliant clarity, and somehow I must make them fold themselves around my overwhelming need. I knew nothing about academic regulations. I did not know how to enroll, or even that I must enroll. I knew only this, very clearly: had life been different, had there been justice, had those invisible powers not hamstrung and double-crossed me, this was the place I would have called mine.

I forced myself to sit very still.

Here I belonged.

A part of me had died in that damp, peeling bathroom less than two hours ago. I felt as raw as a snake that had just shed its skin. A ripple could undo me. My heart held dread—sweet dread for a change. From these steps I would fashion a brand new beginning. By what means? I would not have known. I would not have known what a college degree was. I did not know that there were different ones, leading to different lifestyles. I had not the faintest idea what I might have to do to obtain one, how long it would take, how much it might cost, what I would do with it once I had earned it, what kind of intellectual rigor might be asked of me, whether or not I was up to it, how I might manage my time to accomplish that mind-boggling feat.

There was a dark polished hall to my right.

At the end of that hall dwelled a dean.

"I am a survivor," I told him.

I sat in his office, totally spent. Sunlight filtered through the windows. A tiny plant grew sparsely in the sunshine, struggling with tips that were raw from the harshness of the soil.

He guessed at my plight from my stuttering plea. He sat there, arms folded, and listened.

I said I was done with my pain.

I said I would no longer lend a hand to pointless torment.

I told him I now rode a wave of sheer determination, and that this wave was climbing, climbing, climbing. He smiled at my fervor. I said that here and now I swore by all that was sacred, to him and to me, that I would rebuild my life, pillar by pillar, and stone by stone, and that he might want to stand nearby and watch me. He smiled at that, too, and opened his hand in a gesture of simple acceptance. I sat in a chair by the door, positioned there in such a way that I had control of the exit. I would not leave without getting an answer. He would not leave until he had shown me the way. He was, after all, a scholarly man who knew all the rules I could not, as yet, even fathom. I told him: "You simply *must* give me permission . . . "

"Permission for what . . . ?" asked he.

Well, that's what I wanted to know. I had no words at all to label my violent hunger. I had no words to put around the vastness of my need.

He said gently: "Just what would you like to study, dear . . . ?"

"Anything. Just anything . . . " I told him fervently.

"Well," he said, clearly impressed, for there was a glint to his glasses. "Why, dear? Just what's the rush? The Draft is hardly after you . . . "

I explained. "No. Not the Draft. It's the Fiend." I well knew my enemy by name.

We stared at each other. His wry remark was lost on me. He did not understand my urgency. But gratefully I knew: This man was on my side. I could sense that. I repeated, to make myself clear: "I would like to study just plain everything."

He said patiently, leaning back into his chair: "Well, study in what subject matter?"

I was groping blindly: "Pardon me . . . ?"

"There are classes and classes. Some are easy. Some are hard. Have you decided on a major yet?"

What was all this war talk? A major was a general of sorts in my befuddled notions—had I found my way into a military school? "I haven't yet talked to a major," I said, swallowing. "But I will, just as soon as I can . . . "

He smiled and said: "Well. Well." His glasses glittered merrily. He said: "You *have* finished high school, I presume?"

I shook my head. "I almost finished eighth grade." That was very much stretching the truth. Counting days and weeks, I had been to school no more than three years. A week here, a week there in bombed-out, war-torn Germany. In this, I was not unique among the Russian-German Mennonites of my decimated generation. Woldi, three years older than I and having caught the force of war much harder, could barely read at all. I, luckier than most, had once gone to a school for the gifted, sponsored by the Allies in a city in Westphalia, in 1946.

In my class, I had been first. But then my mother had resettled in the jungle, and there an elder's zealous ire put a stop to my formal schooling before I turned fourteen.

I said: "I can read anything. I can manage easily—I know that I can."

"I'm afraid you don't speak English well enough to manage easily."

"I can learn."

"Really?"

"Yes, really. Believe me I can."

"How? What will you do?"

I said: "What will *you* do? For I'm not leaving."

I sat in his chair, stiffening my spine. Let him go get the police. Let him get horses and chains to drag me away. I knew myself well. I had exhausted all my previous choices, all the reserves from which I could draw. If I did not replenish myself, I would as surely die as that thirsting plant in that sunflooded window. I would not return to my hell. I knew that simple certainty with every fiber of my being. I would not leave without gaining some anchor of sorts—a rational, reasoning guideline that would somehow help me get hold of my pain.

I must have looked determined, for he, with raised eyebrows, said after a pause: "Well, what the heck! What the heck! Why don't you try some English classes? Some writing, perhaps, to help you get up to speed? I'm sure that somewhere there's a spot for you, my dear, in Academia . . . "

I did not know what to make of his words, but I sensed his good will—very strongly. This was a good, kind, generous man who told me, leaning forward: "Let's face it, honey. There's no way you can survive in our regular degree-granting programs. But a class or two in Adult Ed? Why not? After all, what can you lose?

"How do I start?"

"Well," said my friend, sunnily, smiling, round-bellied archangel guarding the gates: "Well, audit some classes. Get a smattering of this and that. You know? A little history? Some anthropology? Perhaps psychology? Something that's easy?

Something that's fun?"

"Oh, thank you! Oh, thank you very, very much!"

"Well, you are very, very welcome. Let me introduce you to our fabled Mrs. Farmer. And our formidable Laura Fox. One is in charge of Continuing Ed. The other one is chief of IBM cards . . . "

CHAPTER TWENTY

The University

I TOOK TO LEARNING like a junkie.

Home I went, that very first day, in an absolute daze of elation, a thumping hammer in my chest: I was admitted to a university! To be honest—I felt like a fraud, an imposter smuggled into the Garden of Eden. Sooner or later, I would be found out.

As I stopped by the grocery store to pick up a gallon of milk, I saw the daily paper. I paid for a copy—I would train my mind in defense. I would start learning formal English by dissecting the meaning of ads. From there, I would inch my way forward.

I did better than that—I discovered Ann Landers. Here was the perfect teaching aid: simple words, a compact message, short vignettes, spicy, lucid stories that were always fun to read, a perfect daily mini-lesson. I cut her out. I stuck her to the door of my refrigerator. For six months, I studied every word she wrote. I studied her for grammar, for idiom, for the intoxicating, puzzling, strange, alluring ways of living in America, a *bona fide* American myself. She became my reliable ally.

New panoramic vistas opened for me.

Fortified with brand new thoughts, I ventured deep into the library. Why, only weeks ago I never even knew a library existed! Now I saw rows and rows of books—miles of books, it seemed to me, all mine, all for the asking. I remember thinking: "If I live to be a hundred years, I can never use them up!" Keep your churches, pious souls. Let me keep my library.

Not that it was easy, at first. I had no trouble reading—I think I was born with the skill and the hunger to read. Writing was a different matter. While I strained to read and listen and absorb, my fingers went on strike—I could not speed my pen. I never did learn taking notes. To this day, I rely on memory.

And English! A brand new, rich and vivid language—but how complicated to untangle without help! I could manage to hang on in casual conversation, but I had no feel at all for English syntax, sentence structure, prepositions, punctuation—anything. If there's a will, there is a way, they say. I came home every day, loaded down with armfuls of hardcover treasures. Every minute I could spare, I immersed my hungry mind in page after page after page. The more I read, the more my inner choking lessened.

Miraculously, Erwin's brain quakes lessened, too. And to my utter disbelief, he managed to hang on in "school."

Erwin's "classroom" was a dusty living room in one of The Academy's back-of-campus cottages. The children sat cramped, elbow to elbow. The teacher was a young black girl—unwashed and ungrammatical, but with unruffled patience and a heart filled with indulgent charity.

"Irving! Irving!" she would cry. "You is funny! You is so funny you crack me up for sure!"

She would lock herself in with the children at a quarter to nine, emerge about noon to disperse her charges for lunch, regather them with clucking tongue at one o'clock, and shush them firmly from her steps at three. I looked around: Beggars can't be choosers. It was a school of sorts all right. There was a blackboard on the wall, a teacher's desk piled high with stacks of unsorted papers, some paper maché, a pot of glue, a pile of unclaimed socks and mittens. The children had desks. Each had a box of crayons. A few of them had pencils with which they jabbed each other in unmitigated combat. Try as I might, I could not see much learning going on.

Once or twice, I tried to observe, but nothing came of that. The teacher took my visit as an invitation for an extended chat, pulled her thermos from her closet, offered to share her curled sandwich with me, and cheerfully let chaos reign. While we "talked," the children attempted to murder each other. It was atrocious—that's all I can say.

I have kept a few of her papers. Here is a sample of "classwork:"

"Dear Valentine: I want you to know this! I like you even more than I like

a) bad breath   b) catching cold   c) my dentist

CIRCLE ONE!

Or, further down the page:

"I wanted to buy you a present but

a) my piggy bank died. And I spent my money on the funeral
b) I have been buying singing lessons for my cat
c) It's hard to find something that still costs only five cents

CIRCLE EITHER A, B, OR C!

Erwin had, as yet, no language! It really wasn't funny. How could he handle "abstractions" like that?

And yet there was a change in Erwin.

He imitated doggedly. He copied spastic nonsense, line after line and page after page. He tried hard, bless his compulsive little soul, swallowing spasmodically, printing page upon page, hour upon hour, day after day. His old, distressing malady had surfaced once again. He could not let go—having been set in a groove, he must stand compelled to continue to copy. I noticed, as I had before, that any word, once copied, was set in Erwin's memory like rock set in cement. His spelling was immaculate. His understanding nil.

I discovered: direction did not matter. He could just as easily spell backwards—it was all the same to him. Not only words. Whole sentences. The clarity of visual recall would stun me. Was there no way to tap into this hidden strength?

To my immense relief, he did not fight going to classes. He never struggled against work—not once. He would grab his pencil like a spear, circling "Yes" and "No," circling "True" and "False." By chance alone, he hit the jackpot now and then. Stickers and stars made him happy. They kept him pushing on.

He started to chant simple singsongs.

He learned some riddles, repeating them over and over, rocking with obvious delight.

Once in a while, he would laugh—a deep, fulfilling belly laugh I did not know his knotted, anguished frame contained. Could mirth reside in his chaotic mind? Was there a place for deep emotions? He clearly seemed to love his teacher and, abundantly, she loved him in return. " . . . Irving! Irving! Stop your shenanigans!" her voice would roll like thunder. I could hear her long before I passed the corner at the chapel on my way to pick him up. She thundered of necessity. She must out-thunder everything—a decrepit air conditioner, the tidal ruckus of "classwork" next door, the lawn mower outside her fly-spattered window, the airplanes that roared overhead. "Stop your shenanigans, I says!"

She never complained about Erwin to me. She scolded him richly at times and cheerfully upbraided him as he deserved and she saw fit, and he would weep with wretchedness, and afterwards, both of them would rock remorsefully as he sought sobbing refuge on her bosom. She took his grotesqueness in stride. She was practical as well, and wholly unapologetic about having to be practical. She would keep him wisely on a leash when walking him around the block for the sake of exercise, decompression, and diversion, and both of them would have a fine and jolly time. " . . . Irving, I swear you is a scream! You is so funny, the way you pull me through the puddles. I swear you is a scream . . . !"

I would avert my eyes and shut my mind. As far as I could see, he did not learn a single useful concept academically. But he did master, crucially and most importantly, a very handy little skill: he learned to sit still in a classroom.

I have debated with myself: should Paul's name be in this book? I am not sure that the debt I owe to this young man can be translated faithfully, much less acceptably. He played a crucial role in the ferment of my awakening, exploratory years, but this he never knew, and I was much too shy and socially inept to tell him. We never shared a hundred private words all through my years of college. That he was there, that he existed, that I could learn from him was a joy and pleasure and discovery to me.

He lectured in psychology — child psychology, to be exact. I thought he was brilliant. Witty. Well-read. A man of easy, nonchalant élan, champion of the underdog, in complete control of his classes. A sea of rapt faces stared up at him from the depths of the immense auditorium where he held his exceedingly popular sessions. Never ever had I seen a room that large, and in it Paul stood, a magician, practicing his sorcery. When he made a clarifying point that shot a zinging bullet through my soul, his words appeared in lighted letters high behind him on a screen. When he spoke, his voice would magnify a dozen times via microphone. He magnified himself by magnifying knowledge — he sprinkled the manna of Heaven for which I had hungered so long.

" . . . learning falls into seven distinct categories: Association. Habituation. Motivation. Variability. Imprinting. Sensitization. Inhibition . . . "

He would send me flying to the dictionary to look up heady words: Association—the connection or relation of ideas. Habituation—to accustom oneself to a given condition by experience or repetition. Sensitization—to become susceptible or hypersensitive to the action of an object or a substance. Inhibition—a checking or restraining; a self-imposed restriction on behavior.

"Yes!" my heart sang out. "That's it! That's it exactly!" Every single word shed light on a past puzzle. Every explanation brought me closer to a goal—to understand my child's assorted, nameless terrors.

"Observation and experiment," said Paul, "are the pillars of hard knowledge . . . " and I could have wept with gratitude, had weeping not detracted precious time from listening to him. A science of the mind, this science of psychology, mine for the asking, and Paul had the key. No voodoo. No prayers. No charlatan nonsense. No empty brotherhood or maudlin milk of human kindness but solid knowledge of parameters that made for solid thought. " . . . the self develops through awareness of one's body. A child's perception of himself has to do with the extent with which he knows that eyes are for sight, and hands are for touching, and ears are meant to sort out sounds that carry meaning. Just the other day, my little four-year-old . . . "

He was a married man, the father of two little boys. They were a little younger than my own. He sometimes weaved an antecdote or two about their funny ways into the magic of his lecture. Every Tuesday and Thursday, there was a new installment of the ways in which they grew. That first semester, I watched Paul and listened to him in absolute, unreserved awe. I would have died had anyone suggested that I might make him notice me. All my emotions careened at the very suggestion. My needs were of a lesser kind, and of a vaster nature.

You might say I had a crush on Paul. But that flip observation does not do my feelings justice.

Every month, the mailman brought our bill for Erwin's education. It was frightening to see it climb so steeply. And for the life of me, I could not pin the very busy Mr. Thompson down to tell me how much we would have to pay, and how much would be covered by the Baton Twirlers' sponsorship that had been promised me. Once I buttonholed an underling. "We'll gladly pay as much as we can, but there's just no way we can pay the entire . . . "

"Look," he said, listening with only half an ear. "Pay something, will you, honey? Give 'em ten bucks. As long as you pay, you show your good will. And just don't always worry . . . "

So we started paying, faithfully but apprehensively, $10.00 on the tenth of each month.

Three times a week, Erwin had "speech" in one of the language therapy rooms. Sometimes, I would watch him furtively through the small square window cut for observation in the door. What he did inside was much of a mystery, too, for the therapist just sat there—or so it seemed to me—scribbling notes or staring into space, while he kept flipping through a magazine and chattering away. Every now and then, she would snap to attention and tell him sternly: " . . . say 'window.' Say 'door' . . . " I knew that he could imitate most any word. He had no difficulty whatsoever imitating language. He talked like a parrot—give him a cue, out popped the response. He could not hook his words to meaning. A crucial link was missing. He was a mystery.

And yet, in time I could detect a subtle change. I could discern his driving need to talk with meaning in the very marrow of my bones. He seemed to want to tell me something—very, very badly. All of a sudden, out of the blue, a burning need to talk was there.

" . . . with language comes thought," lectured Paul. "Without language, a child cannot think very smoothly . . . " He lectured with the ease of erudition within the very boundaries whose mysteries I longed to break. I was sure he knew the answers, and he would teach them all to me. "Give a youngster words to use, and you have set him on the path to reason . . . "

He was, perhaps, in his mid-twenties — full of sagacity and tease. He was young, and I was ancient. He was smart, and I was dull. He was keen, and I was empty. I was wooden; he had flair. My grief had made me blind and deaf, and he had piercing understanding. He was an oracle to me.

He was a radical of sorts — a rebel in search of a cause. "Let's wage war against hypocrisy," he said, and I, a believer, felt raw emotions clog my nose. Yes, I agreed that knowledge should be relevant. I, too, would risk my neck for principles. No, life was not a vale of tears. We did have, after all, some options. Let the chips fall where they may. Life should be pleasure. Fun. Happiness. Joy. We were not born to drudgery.

I longed to shed my unbearable burden, and there were moments — sweet, frivolous moments — when I was sure I could. When I walked, dazed, out of his classes, past the sun-tanned, jean-clad youngsters almost half my age, down to the cafeteria to take a coffee break, I felt the spring air settle gently in my hair.

CHAPTER TWENTY-ONE

New Vistas

I SPLIT MY SOUL in two.

I was two people now—one young and free and eager to be tutored, the other cowed and burdened and downtrodden, a captive dunce. The prisoner cooked dinners, washed clothes, rinsed the dust and paint and grease from Woldi's pants. The unfettered "me" delved into the labyrinth of bookshelves, Xeroxed papers, spent heady afternoons in luxurious pursuit of a footnote—a happy devotee set on the track of mysteries.

"Life's sweetest lessons can't be found in books," said Paul.

Before I stepped onto this different plane and planet, I had assumed that classwork was austere. Paul convinced me otherwise. Often the entire class would settle into trivial chitchat. At other times, it all but bristled with the sparks of Paul's fine, questing mind. He was shrewd. He was savvy. He would parry every question with a question of his own. "Let's be open. Let's experiment." He would utter strong commandments: " . . . Break with your past. Be true to yourself. Be authentic . . . " That was very heady stuff for me. He wore elbow patches every girl in class considered sexy. How I envied them for their ease of manners, for their dusty braided sandals and their long unruly hair. They fell all over him, the wicked things. They flirted. They teased. Their glances spoke a coded language all their own. I only longed to have him for a friend. He and I would bump into each other accidentally. He would invite me for a chat; we would linger over coffee. I would call him, without flinching, by first name.

I never fantasized beyond this point. That would have been preposterous. But I was keenly aware of the sparks of his presence. I felt his pull in every fiber, every pore.

The following year, a young and zealous woman replaced Erwin's well-meaning but pedagogically dubious teacher. This one came saturated once again with the spirit of the righteous—a born-again Baptist, as I recall, who put me under scrutiny at once, found me sorely lacking, and therefore offered pointedly to pray for me. To my amazement, I discovered tolerance. I found I need no longer jump on everybody who as much as looked at me askew.

I had to admit: this new teacher knew exactly how to teach. She knew a great deal about children like Erwin. She insisted that he behave acceptably or be dismissed, no tears, please! for the day. She taught him to raise his hand before speaking. She insisted that he speak only if, as she put it, " . . . he really has something to say."

I said: "Why, that's impossible. He does not speak with meaning . . . he never has, not yet."

"It's time that he learned," she told me briskly. "That's no dummy you have here."

For that I could have hugged her. And Erwin did not seem to mind the rigor and the discipline. That summer, wonder of wonders, he started to read.

Of course he had, for close to half his life, been capable of memorizing words. This teacher taught from the assumption that he would learn to tie meaning to sensory cues. Every day she hauled in cards and finger paints and toys and clay and made him feel and taste and smell the shape of meaning. She insisted that he read for meaning, or not bother to read at all. He would be soaked with perspiration from his effort. She would only say: "All right. That wasn't so bad. Now try again."

She taught him techniques to keep himself under control. She would tell him sternly: "Keep your cool. Start all over!" She bridled his panic. She sensitized him to his long and painful chain of nonsense words. At times, I thought her far too harsh and too demanding and unfair. Far too controlling. Far too intolerant of his puzzling limitations. After all, he could not really see or hear or feel as she and I.

I did not realize that I had reached a crossroad of sorts. Yes, there were limits to capacity, for damage to his central nervous system had deprived him of some crucial learning when he was small and should have learned. My child had missed developmental milestones. Once chronological milestones were by-passed, all learning was slow and impaired. Paul had lectured on that very point the other day.

I went beyond. Deep down a voice spoke up that I had never heard before. This voice insisted that, perhaps, it was too late altogether. Perhaps there was no catching up, not any more, once central nervous system damage had occurred and too much time had passed. It was a nagging little voice. It was weak. But it was there.

In the beginning, as I felt my way through the maze of a huge university, I was a timid soul. I did not mix with fellow students for fear I would be found a fraud. One wrong move would cause eviction. The Archangel Gabriel would summon me out.

In my sophomore year, I did raise my hand in some classes. To my astonishment, my answer was not odd, the world still turned, no one took notice, life went on. That experience left me shaken. So depleted was I of a meaningful "me" that the slightest sip of inner independence could easily undo me, unravel me, lay bare the ignoramus I knew myself to be. Yet my grades were so high that, in my junior year, I was asked to join

Phi Kappa Phi. I was touched by the beautiful and poignant initiation. Afterwards, a fellow student—a handsome boy no more than half my age—took me by the hand and led me through a crowd of fellow honor students, as if I were an equal, to introduce me to a friend. The natural gesture bewitched me. I felt cherished for the first time in my life for my intelligence. It took little, in those days, to make my starved self drunk with joy.

In 1969, as one-fifth of mankind watched America reach for the moon, I watched Erwin reach for the very beginnings of meaningful language.

One day he came home and lay on the floor and struggled and twisted and strained. "What is it?" I asked, watching torrents of excitement run like lava up and down his muscle-knotted thighs. "*Schatzi,* try to tell me what you really want to say . . . " I had learned, as mothers will, to read his wants by intuitive means. That day I knew he had something very important to tell me.

He rolled himself into a curl. A heartbreak look, beseechingly. Mumbo jumbo.

"Try again," I said, having learned.

He shuddered.

"Again."

He turned purple from the effort. He all but gurgled with his need. He rolled his eyes and wrung his hands and slapped himself in agony. I took hold of both his temples. I cradled them within my palms, feeling his pulse through his surgical scars in the tips of my own throbbing fingers.

"Again."

"P . . . p . . . pre . . . tty."

At that, he broke into copious tears.

I squatted by his side, watching him with awe. So much energy for just a single word? He seemed totally spent, as if he had climbed the steepest of mountains. He heaved a deep and heartfelt sigh. He fell asleep—a coma-like sleep that came after one of the "seizures" that had plagued him so in infancy. It lasted five minutes, perhaps. I waited, holding him gently. Then he woke, surprisingly refreshed. He took a deep breath and said it again, this time with much less effort:

"Pretty . . . Mom."

"What is pretty, *Schatzi?* Can't you tell me what you mean?"

He struggled free of me.

Very early next morning, all warm and flannel-cuddly, he climbed into bed with me, whispering into my ear: "Pretty . . . Mommy . . . no?"

"Pretty what?" I asked.

I swear he gave me a conspiratorial smile. For a tiny fleeting moment, my monster-child looked impish—he did, I swear! For a second or two, he actually focused his eyes. He flung away my blankets. He seemed impatiently eager to make it to school.

" . . . pretty!" he shouted and waved and wobbled away.

He came home in the late afternoon. He was carrying something with very great care. He had wrapped it with some tissue paper, awkwardly. Tears shot into my lids. My knotted, twisted, flailing Frankenstein stood there, on tiptoes, handing me a present—very, very gingerly.

"Pretty. Mom. You. Me."

I still have it. It hangs in my entrance next to my office front door. Visitors will "ohhh" and "ahhh" with politeness and wonder what it signifies. To the untutored eye, it may be a ceramic disc of simple, arabesque design—clay poured into a form, baked in a kiln to glazed constancy, a little smudgy at the edges, the colors blurred. It's more. It is intelligence fashioned from chaos.

Erwin looked at his work of creation with rapture.

"Pretty," he said, simply. "Mommy-don't-you-think-so-too . . . ?"

CHAPTER TWENTY TWO

The Light of Heart

ONCE LANGUAGE CAME, it came in leaps and bounds. At first, it was woefully garbled, but soon I could discern some reasons as to why my little heartbreak stood compelled to throw wrong switches all the time.

"Whenever Dad sneezes," he told me one day, "he makes me dizzy in my head."

"Don't cough. You break my ears to pieces," he told Rudy.

One day he declared: "My head is too little for Christmas."

When I worked with him on his homework, he would work to saturation and not a step beyond. "No more room in my eyes," he would say, and push me away.

"Cursive writing doesn't fit my brain," he said when he was twelve. "If I push it in, it feels funny." He did not learn to write in cursive hand until he was almost a man.

Recently I sat with him in my kitchen, and I said: "I am writing a book about you. Can you tell me how you felt when you were little?"

Here is part of what he dictated to me:

" . . . I was just crazy when I was small. I didn't like it too much. It made lots of tension in my head. My brain was moving. Snakes were in the jam in the basement. My head was going up and down. The bones in my head were going up and down. It felt like they were going to break. When I couldn't talk, it was silent in my throat. It felt as if my brain was someplace else . . . "

"Let's take a lie," lectured Paul. "A lie requires higher-order integration. To tell a lie means going against one's better judgment of reality—we negate reality when we decide to lie . . . "

Such explanations fit Erwin to a dot.

For the very life of him, Erwin could not tell a lie. To this day, he cannot say: " . . . the grass is red . . . " for that is contrary to his better knowledge, a violation of his repertoire of "facts."

Once he broke my cherished coffee mug.

"Where is my cup?" I asked.

He put both fists to his ears: "Why are you asking me who broke your cup? Don't ask who broke your cup. Look under my pillow."

"Did you break it and hide it under your pillow?"

Utterly astonished: "How did you know?"

He could not handle any form of make-believe. He did not care for Santa Claus, or Easter bunnies, or the Munster family on TV. Once I contracted a stubborn case of laryngitis and could only speak in whispers for two weeks. I scared the living daylights out of Erwin: "Mommy! Mommy! Are you a ghost . . .?" He kept a close and anxious watch on me for days.

Family relationships troubled him to the point of retching nausea:

"If he's your husband," he would say, screwing up his face at Woldi, "is he my husband, too?"

"No. Daddy is your father."

"Then he's your father, too?"

"No, but he is Rudy's father."

"And Rudy's husband?"

"No, he is only Rudy's father."

"Is Rudy a husband to me?"

Round and round, in circles, we would travel. He could not grasp family order and has much trouble with such abstract concepts to this day. At age fourteen, he wrote me his very first letter. "Dear Mrs. Rimland," he let it be known, "this is Erwin Rimland writing . . . "

Paul was a fiery champion against an array of social ills, and we spent many sessions assailing this and that: the war in Vietnam, the racial mix of schools, the draft, the obstacles against the open sale of contraceptives, abuses of the welfare state. I could not quite connect all that to child psychology, and I felt strongly drawn as well as offended. I marvelled at the passions Paul aroused. But students—an exploited class? Computers—our enemies? The system—out to get me? Maudlin sentiments, all that! I had my memories of mud huts and mosquitos. This place, with its cool spaciousness and polished halls and soft drink dispensers was a place far to be preferred.

I experienced the upheavals of the Sixties as an alien from outer space. Yet I felt every nuance, every thrill and beat and dive and pitch surging through the halls of my beloved university where I sat, now a legitimate student, yellow pad, books, ball point pen and all, and marvelled at my transformation. Through the plate glass window I could see The Radicals, handing out leaflets, circulating petitions. The university—out to dehumanize me? What utter childish nonsense! Could anybody solve injustice by holding hands and gushing love and munching chips? By golly—no sit-ins for me. I judged them with the harshness of a Solzhenitzyn who had known, first hand, the Gulag Archipelago. Not a shred had I in common with these spoiled and lazy youngsters, with their Levis torn and faded so as to signify exactly where they stood—on the side of "justice and equality," fair and square against their country's "moral bankruptcy." I thought their causes petty and contrived compared to all the struggles I had known. They could not ever share my reverence of education, my hunger for the riches of the mind. Let them cop out. I wanted in.

Once a girl had herself arrested for creating a disturbance at a downtown freedom school. She had participated in some leftist demonstration and had spent the night in jail. She was released just in the nick of time to make it to our session. Classmates circled her with envy. Paul treated her with reverence.

"Tear gas?" queried Paul.

"Well, no . . . " the girl admitted sadly. Paul looked sorely disappointed. She hung her head in shame that she had let him down.

"Martin Luther King's been shot," wept one girl one evening, expecting me to join her in a hastily arranged symbolic wake. I shook her off. Martin Luther Who? I had enough wails of my own.

"My own priorities are different," I told her haughtily, never missing using yet another ornamental word. My own priorities *were* different. I had to go home to shorten the hem of my dress.

I earned "A" upon "A" upon "A" in Paul's classes. I knew that Paul handed out grades only under duress, yielding to administrative mandate. Along with other bourgeois vices, Paul eschewed the grading system, since it went against his grain of overall equality and brotherhood. But to me, these "A's" meant much. Sometimes he would decorate my paper with a scribbled comment: "I enjoy your writing very much. Your essay on the Doman-Delacato method shows fine understanding of attempts to retrieve lost brain cells via patterning . . . "

At such times, my heart could not contain my bliss.

The Doman-Delacato method was yet another rainbow I had decided to pursue. I think I read about its sweeping claims in the paper. A team of "specialists" alleged that, via "baby exercises" such as creeping, crawling, and cross-patterning, it was possible to make a damaged brain find neural pathways around its areas of injury. They claimed that parents could re-teach a child "from scratch" by taking him through infancy: put him on the floor and work him over systematically, force the brain to "grow new tissue" through massive repetitive sensory input.

"Get yourself a team of volunteers," the battle cry went forth. "Move the child's arms and legs back and forth, back and forth, cross-body-wise, left arm and right leg, right arm and left leg, for hours, days, and months at a time . . . " Even now, similar claims tend to pop up in the papers. The theory has never been fully accepted within the professions—or, for that matter, disproven. It still claims stout disciples. I feel ambivalent about it to this day.

Anyway, at the time it seemed novel and promising, but where was I to get close to a hundred volunteers? One day, as I sat in my favorite club chair during a break between classes, watching yet another signing of petitions, it suddenly occurred to me: could I not tap into this youthful willingness and strength?

Thus it happened that, one fine and balmy morning, I planted myself at the stairs of the recreation area with a handful of flyers in my hand to solicit social action on behalf of my handicapped child.

They volunteered in droves. At all hours of the day and night, they would come zooming up into my driveway with their jalopies, stride along my outside hall on bare and dusty feet, roll and somersault Erwin the length of my living room carpet, pummel him across the lawn with countless chin-ups, push-ups, and sit-ups, promenade with him on Maple Street so he could "walk the curb," or quietly sit with him and stroke his back to "stimulate his nerve ends." They would take him swimming or fishing or hiking or on long walks along the dry river bed. They rubbed his wrists and dangled coins before his eyes. They made him breathe into a paper bag—all this supposedly for therapeutic reasons. They told him jokes and taught him songs of peace and brotherhood and quite a few four-letter words, and loved him half to death with their cheerful zeal and ardor.

I was amazed at their persistence and their diligence. This

was serious business — far better than the study of some dry and dusty classic! Each day, after school, they would pick Erwin up according to a complicated, ritualistic schedule they kept in tattered copies in their carefully shrunk jeans, and he would gurgle with delight and creep and crawl and jump, and they would stand and cheer him on and chart his progress on a bar graph. Education must be relevant! They were convinced that they could make him well, although by then not even I could quite believe that.

I can't say whether or not Erwin learned to think more smoothly as a result of months of Doman-Delacato patterning, but he blossomed with attention and picked up a lot of useful social skills. These children of the Sixties put their eagerness around his fractured mind, and I am sure that it became a brace on which he structured later learning.

One day they decided that Erwin should jump rope.

I thought: "That is impossible."

His sense of balance had always been woefully poor. He still struggled with a spoon. He still could not focus his eyes. Riding a bike was entirely out of the question. His dozen arms and legs still flailed like so many flapping windmills. He would trip on an eyelash, as folklore might say. But patiently his friends decided that the mastery of jumping rope was something that was now imperative, and they would cheer him on, help him count, jump along with him if needed, and soon he could manage ten, twelve, fifteen rope beats at a time.

I noticed: Exercises seemed to burn some poison, seemed to clear his brain. He would walk on tiptoes after patterning and chant and hum and smile. This made me brood for days about the link between his inability to learn and biochemistry. These days one reads about the "highs" that joggers claim. They have a point, I'm sure. A good sweat made my child euphoric.

One day, after a vigorous session, he came to me and looked at me with a clear, razorsharp, riveting look. I have forgotten what he said. But I shiver even now recalling what I saw — an unimpeded pathway to his soul. I will think of that moment, always, with heartbreak and longing. A keen intelligence was there — a nugget deeply buried. Our eyes have never met like that again. But I still see his glance, now and then, sharp and questing and engrossing, in my dreams and in my nightmares.

CHAPTER TWENTY THREE

Tunnel's End

ON THE TENTH OF EACH MONTH, we received The Academy's bill. It now stretched to thousands of dollars. Each month we made our token payment. We could have, and would have, paid more. But by then my heart had learned to speak the language of dissent: this was, supposedly, a land of freedom and equality. Was not every child entitled to a free education—a right that came to others at their birth? Why should we have to pay so much?

We had sold our home in Canada and had purchased a small house in the better part of town, but the payments and the taxes and past bills to hospitals in Canada still kept us strapped. The equity in our home was less than half of what we owed to The Academy. To pay for Erwin's schooling would yoke us for a lifetime.

And here was still that nagging voice: was it worth it after all? He had come arduous distances. But he was getting older. Could he catch up? Rudy had out-distanced him by far.

I had plowed doggedly through preliminary fields in child psychology: psychometrics, probability theory, pigeons and their reinforcement charts. I discovered many warring schools of thought, but once I had mastered the tedious footwork, or so I had assumed, I would come upon the master key. For most of my life, I had felt alternately murderous and suicidal. Reading made me feel a calm, directed peace. I could find out, once and for all, what could and could not be done. According to my findings, I would then chart my strategies.

I poured over books with a hunger that never let up. *Psychological Foundations of Education. Curriculum Development. Differential Approaches to Remediation. Educating Exceptional Children. Intermediate Statistics. Psychological Tests and Measurements.* Every book a labyrinth of wonder, awe, and mystery to me, a beckoning gate to deeper understanding.

The library became my church. Awash with gratitude, I would worship science and the powers of the mind. In a trance I would work, many a night, until eleven o'clock arrived and the doors to my paradise closed. And walking out, question upon question churning in my mind, I would step into the soft, still night and know that I was happy. Or very nearly so.

I told Paul with hammering heartbeat: "Like you, I want a doctorate in child psychology."

"We know so little about the science of behavior and emotions," said Paul, and winked at a passing coed. "And much of what we know is scattered."

He was right—I saw that more and more. There was no real coherence to psychology. Scattered flashes here and there, but no master plan, no map. But no matter how much pioneering it would take, I was ready, eager, capable and willing. I would bring my passions to the field. Whatever nuggets might be hidden in the world's prestigious universities, I would find them, dig them up, shovel by shovel, and haul them to the schools. I would harness all accumulated knowledge, amass it, digest it, condense it, order it and channel it to ease for other parents the burden of their battle.

" . . . This is the story of the child who cannot learn. Every teacher has encountered him. Many a parent, griefstricken and

helpless, has had to cope with him. Every community, sooner or later, will have to deal with him . . . "

True—it was just a tiny editorial. But it was accepted right away. I was now a published writer. Nobody I had known had ever published anything.

It was a heady thing—my first printed byline over an article written in English. Why had I ever thought that life had washed me up? That I was finished as a functioning and thinking human being? Who had dared to make me feel that way?

"Hardened erroneous beliefs," I wrote to clarify matters, "are called stereotypes. Once formed, attitudes are very resistant to change. Prejudices are preserved and supported by the needs they help satisfy. Societies protect themselves—segregation and inferior positions are assigned to people of conflicting points of view . . . "

All right. It does sound pompous. But then it made a bridge. It stood for insight. It cleared those cobwebs from my mind.

I now began to understand the power that comes with unyielding cultural norms: like spider's secretions, sectarian life had paralyzed me because I was a threat; I challenged the existing order. So there! I had that boxed in neatly now. I left my papers scattered on the kitchen table. Let Woldi dare to push them out of the way.

At home, silences thickened. Silences stretched over days at a time. In the morning, Woldi would leave, slamming doors. I would heave a sigh of great relief. Rudy went off on his bike—he was in fourth grade now, a friendly, independent child who hardly needed me at all—and I would hastily pack Erwin's lunch, load all his arms and legs into my car, and drop him off as well: a burden shed for the day! Another left turn, a sweep across the parking lot, a short brisk walk, and I stood in another world—a world where I was valued, where I stood very tall.

Woldi and I drifted apart. I liked the feeling of release that came with inner detachment. Once I had loved him very much, without reserve and recompense. Now I avoided his nearness. Fool's paradise had been my love. He and I were waging silent, bitter war. He slouched, an enemy of joy and life, across from me. He frowned at my essays; he hated my books. In front of the children, he would make fun of me. He was a drag, a dawdler. He unravelled at the fringes of my heaven. He poked along while I, an eagle, soared. It was not within his means, I grimly told myself, to understand the vastness of the distance that a word—a single word that clarified—could put between our souls.

I saw in his confusion at my metamorphosis, his plain perplexity at what was happening right in his house, the blind hostility to anything and anybody different that had so plagued me as a child. I now began to understand, I told myself, the extraordinary violence done to my youth, done to my many possibilities. Not all that long ago, I had been a youngster voracious for meaning and knowledge—I must have seemed marked to "them" from the start. I had not chosen "them." "They" had not chosen me. "They" had tried to force upon my pliant mind their unfair absolutes. Fluke and circumstance—that's what it was. I had tried—God, had I tried!—but still "they" mocked uniqueness, talent, Me. To my eternal pride, I had not settled for their petty world. And since their world—their strange, unpitying, merciless, narrow sectarian world—could not lay claim to me, it had, via twisted detours, laid claim to the mind of an innocent child. I read the diabolical design in its entirety. I now saw its smoldering malice. And I was married for life, I told myself savagely, right unto death, to one of their own.

I don't recall just when that moment came when, overwhelmingly, I hungered to know who "they" really were. From whence had come their strength? What made my life so difficult, what made me so abrasive, why could I not adjust and be a pliant soul and play the pious role assigned to me?

And it so happened — providentially? — that right within my reach, not forty miles from where I lived, was housed the largest collection of Mennonite writings in the entire world. One hot and muggy afternoon, I took myself upon a secret expedition. I checked into a basement library to read up on my past.

For all his limitations, Erwin had access to uncanny channels of "knowledge" deep within his tortured brain. Out of the blue he would announce: "On Wednesday I'll be sick . . . " and sure enough, come Wednesday, he was sick, the little rogue! Sometimes I felt resentful; I felt he led me on. I was convinced he did it just to spite me.

I was ashamed of my own ambivalence. Was my never-ending hope and patience running out? Was I beginning to resent my child? But fevers? Headaches? Nausea? How could he tell ahead of time? Yet sick he was, and sick he remained, the rascal, until something within him would snap: " . . . by Sunday I'll be well." Come Sunday, his temperature would plummet.

To this day, he has retained this power of forecasting illness, although it is not as reliable as it was at the threshold of thought. I don't know on what subconscious powers he draws. Can he sense an illness about to invade? How can he gauge its length? Does he program himself, or does he just report on what his inner radar tells him? He'll only shrug: "Inside me I just know."

Another facet of his extraordinary strength of memory for trivia surfaced early — his obsessive knack for anchoring details of time to insignificant events. Just recently I had the following exchange with him:

"Mom, remember the shampoo bottle that you bought on Friday, August 16th, 1968?"

"No. What about it?"

"I lost the cap. On Sunday, August 18th, at 10:30 a.m. Daylight Savings Time."

He once had a teacher with whom he would play games:

"Do you remember what you did on Thursday, April 22, at 1:45 p.m.?"

"No. What did I do, Erwin?"

"You wrote 'asparagus.' "

Sometimes, even now, we play parlor games. We'll ask him: "On what day did the sixth of July fall in 1965?"

Without hesitation: "On a Tuesday."

He could function at a higher level than anyone had dared to hope. He began to develop reliable patterns. I could leave him alone for hours at a time watching The Flintstones or copying homework, without having to anticipate a strangulation with a coat hanger or a near drowning in a shower or, as happened once, a fingertip caught in a door, and no one there to free him. Much of his bizarre behavior ceased. He could sit still in mannerly fashion. I had a child, almost, like any other child.

Or did I?

The old refrain. He had come far. I was no longer all that sure that I could take him farther.

I have a handful of notes, written at that time:

" . . . his first real project: took a box, cut two square holes, one round hole, and a slit, put a rubber band around it, and pretended that it was a camera . . . "

" . . . played by himself in the sand box. Made two lakes, and a river in between . . . "

" . . . worked on a 100-piece puzzle all afternoon . . . "

I recorded this conversation: "Mother, how does the air conditioner stop?"

"When the room gets hot enough, it stops. See this little metal tongue? It has to go to 75 . . . "

"Yes, but how does it *stop?* Does it have a key, like a car?"

Or at another time:

"Mom, how does a mountain get made?"

Me, drawing on introductory geology: "It grows from the ground. Just like a tree."

Erwin, thoughtfully: "Watch me! I'll get me a mountainseed. I'll grow me my very own mountain . . . "

But also:

" . . . had to pry the evening paper from his teeth . . . "

" . . . caught him in the middle of the night. Totally disoriented. Confused the refrigerator with the bathroom. Was just about to pee into my lettuce box . . . "

" . . . setback in language. Mumbo jumbo. Not a single word that makes much sense . . . "

" . . . episodes of heavy stuttering . . . "

" . . . when angry, gets blue in the face. Twitchings that look like convulsions . . . "

" . . . bit Rudy in the thigh . . . "

Of all the ironies! I had run far. And here I was, thumbing through old documents, searching for a means to write a scathing novel of the Mennonites and their destructive ways.

"I'll show them!" I said at first, contemptuously. Then I said: "You're kidding . . . " And then I fell silent, and just read on and on.

I read through an entire summer. To my immense surprise, my view of Mennonites began to shift.

As novices will, I wrote an autobiographical first draft. I abandoned it almost at once. To write about myself alone was too restricting to the ethnic themes I now began to dip up from the dust of centuries.

I realized I had seen life among the Mennonites in small, restricting captions. I now began to see a people singularly uniform—identical memories in home after home, identical faces, identical joys, identical sorrows. The world, they said in unison, would come to doom, were it not for the prayers of a people such as they. That's all they had left—a handful of language-impoverished prayers! Every cell in my body revolted, responding to the old unmuted pain. But I began to see a different picture. Here was a story larger, much larger than my own.

The Wanderers became my catalyst.

There is much to the Mennonite pacifist story, too rich in hues, too intricate to be recounted here. Let me just say that I began to see a badly decimated people with whom I could identify, who needed to cling to their unwritten rules of faith and devotion—for otherwise could even one of them have managed to survive at all? A simple, odd, diligent people, intermarried over centuries, cutting their furrows, seeding their grain—that was my unknown Russian-German ancestry? The maelstrom of two wars. Destruction. Death. Siberia. The slaughter of their males. The torch put to their homesteads. The holocaust, both sky and earth, both East and West, both from within and from without—through no fault of their own. To be small, to be humble, to be inconspicuous, to fold one's hands and claim all evil was God's will to test the right and righteous, made for survival—of body, heart, and soul.

I was never so engrossed. I read and read and read.

The best of once-strong intellectual leadership these people left behind—in unmarked graves, in icy tombs, in the craters, in the rubble and the ashes of a defeated Europe. A few who scrambled out—and don't ask by what means or at what price!—were dumped by zealous brethren in the jungle, where they lived their small and squalid lives, said heartfelt grace for every sandy bowl of soup, and died a small and squalid death, and that was that, no questions asked or answered. And there I found myself, a bird of a flamboyant plumage—for only the strongest, the best of their young had survived! No wonder that I frightened oldsters with my fire and my zeal! I now began to understand why Ohm Jasch, a preacher with a sparrow's brain, had taken delight in tormenting me, had prevented my mother from teaching . . .

Ohm Jasch! I had my villain now. I soon had my protagonists.

I shed page after page after page.

I felt like a climber of mountains. While perched on stony surfaces, searching for a foothold, always seeing depth below, I had not seen the quiet splendor of the kaleidoscopic ethnic landscape that had surrounded me. Apart from it, I saw its majesty. While living with the Mennonites, I had never known a sense of inner dignity. Apart from them, I understood. At last alone, I stood released.

And while I knew that Mennonites, collectively, would have proved lethal to my soul, a tiny nagging voice now queried: "Perhaps one day—a tacit truce? With some?"

Almost from the start, I knew: *The Wanderers* is a novel that will count.

CHAPTER TWENTY FOUR

The Baton Twirlers

IN THE SPRING OF THE following year, we began to get threatening letters: Pay up, or face legal action.

I called The Academy's lawyer, a man who had become my friend.

"Don't worry," he said kindly. "These letters are only routine."

The letters continued. They were not pleasant letters to receive. Again I called. Again I was reassured.

One day there came a telegram. It scared me out of my wits. Twenty-four hours, or so I read the message, or I would land in jail.

I pushed my books aside and sat down with pencil and paper. Woldi earned at that time, as I recall, a little over $2.00 per hour. I was on scholarships and student loans. Our debt had reached thousands of dollars. Even if we sold our house, even if I stopped my classes and joined the typing pool again, even if I worked my fingers to the bone for two lifetimes in a row, I could not repay the money that we owed to The Academy. I crept into bed, ten thousand knots in my stomach. I could not close an eye that night. Beside me, Woldi snored.

Early next morning, as soon as I could, I drove to The Academy in search of my good Mr. Thompson to remind him once again of what he had promised me.

Mr. Thompson, I found out, was gone.

A successor sprawled in his chair, a young chap with a flashy tie and very supercilious manners. I took a deep breath and recounted, yet one more time, the tale of my financial woes. I told him that I had been promised, many times, that arrangements with the Baton Twirlers of Ontario would be made that would help us pay for Erwin's education. "Erwin's name is on their list . . . "

"What list?" asked the stranger, twirling his pencil. "I know of no such list."

"I have discussed it many times with Mr. Thompson . . . "

He said, derision in his glance: "Let me ask you this: Can you pay? If you can, there's no problem."

"How much?"

"Why, all that you owe us, of course. For a start, why don't you start paying . . . "

I can't recall the monthly amount that he named. I do remember that a frantic calculation whirred through my head. Thirty weeks of Woldi's pay. More than two-thirds off the top of his earnings.

"I couldn't possibly . . . "

Could The Academy function on air? the chap with the flashy tie wanted to know. This was a business like any other business. Had they not given me credit for over two years? Could I not work as well? I was going to school? Taking what? Macrame?

I went straight to the university and, shaking like a leaf, cancelled all my classes. Then I went home and shook some more.

A second mailgram came that night.

I lay on cold sheets, staring into the darkness. Had I come to my surrender point? And was it even worth it? And yet . . . and yet . . . I could not let them kick my little misfit out. Who would make room for him? Where would he go? Where would *we* go? We had no place to go.

I placed a long distance call to the President of the Baton Twirlers of America. Yes, it was urgent. Pertaining to what? Pertaining to a list. Would someone, please, find time to talk to me? Would someone check to see if such a masterlist existed? If Erwin's name was on that list?

"Just a minute," said the neutral voice. "I'll talk to someone. I'll call you right back."

I sat by the telephone and waited and waited. In the late afternoon, I went out to pick up a paper and study the want-ads. What could I do? Wash windows? Scrub floors?

The next morning, around ten, just as I was about to go and sell my soul to Fuller Brush or Tupperware, the mailman rang the bell to hand me a speeded, certified letter.

With trembling fingers, I tore the envelope open.

It contained a kindly personal reply on Baton Twirlers' stationery, wrapped into a flyer of sorts: ". . . I am informing the parties concerned regarding this situation, so that steps can be taken to set your mind at ease . . . we have assumed responsibility for a third child, Evan, whose family position is similar to yours . . . there is little doubt in my mind that something can be worked out, but first we must have all the facts . . . "

I read on with swimming eyes. Included were two documents. One was a rather simpering letter, bearing The Academy's logo, soliciting funds for "Evan"—whose history and whose assorted maladies matched Erwin's, point by point. It quoted "Evan's" mother. I stared at it. Why, I had written that! The other was an open letter written by the chairman of the Baton Twirlers' Scholarship Fund, an urgent appeal to all members living in Ontario to make an extra effort, to pitch in with " . . . ten cents per day," to approach friends, clubs, employers, unions . . . I could not believe what I saw! More than a year ago, all across Ontario, kind people had donated time and effort and money to help pay for "Evan's" school — and I had never known!

I drove straight to the Academy. I said, my voice that of a stranger: "Where is the money?" I said: "Somebody has this money in his pocket . . . " I said: "I will take this story to the papers." I said: "How dare you torment me like that!" At that, I started to cry.

What can I say?

They sat me down and made me listen. A mix-up in names. A regrettable misunderstanding. Mr. Thompson was no longer here. Nobody could explain just what happened, just why he kept his records as he did. Sloppily, no doubt. Mistakes did happen, wasn't that true? They happened to the best of people. And did I not agree that Erwin's progress was astounding — why would I want to stir up dust? A stupid little paperwork error. I could forgive a bureaucratic error — could I not? Could I try to see this matter from a much harassed, brand new administrator's point of view?

I could, and I did.

Parents of handicapped children, in those days, did not have many choices. And what do I know even now? For all I know, it might have been just sloppiness. Let's say it was just sloppiness. I never followed up on it. I never did receive another bill. And, yes, it was true, I agreed — on good days Erwin counted all the way to fifty.

CHAPTER TWENTY FIVE

My-Very-Own-Bike

ON GOOD DAYS. On bad days, he could still be horrible. With this latest blow, I had reached a state of profound inner conflict. The betrayal simply demoralized me. And doubt about the merits of our struggle kept eating away at my efforts. I talked to myself quite brutally now. I said to myself: "He's retarded. He will never change. He might improve, but he won't change. He will always be different. He will always be odd."

I had read a thousand books, and more. Not one of them spelled hope.

I said to myself: "He is eleven now, going on twelve."

I said to Woldi: "We have Rudy. He is entitled to a childhood, too." I said: "What about us? Our marriage is no marriage any more."

To avoid my choking, passionate speeches, Woldi would leisurely take himself fishing.

I took count. Erwin now did many things that once had seemed impossible. He could jump without crumbling at the knees. We could take him to a restaurant, and we could take him to the library where he would sit and read. He could read quite well, and he could write cute simple letters. His control of language varied—sometimes it was badly garbled, and sometimes it was crystal clear. I would help him practice by the hour, and Woldi was endlessly patient with him, deepening the furrows I had plowed. During free time, Erwin trailed in Rudy's wake, and while he could not mix with other children and often there were ugly teasings, Rudy did not seem to mind and would stand up for him. We all did what we could, but it was difficult, and there were times of real resentment. He was a deep and painful thorn in our side. Although we did not say so, we longed to yank it out.

There was one thing that Erwin could not do: he could not ride a bicycle.

He owned a bike—a sore point of contention for many struggling years. We had bought it for him right after we returned from Germany when Rudy had been five years old and had asked for an " . . . honest-to-goodness two-wheeler." A bike, to us, was a fortune in those days. To buy two brand new bikes seemed just about impossible.

"Rudy is entitled to his bike," I had tried to reason with my spouse, "but there's no possible way that Erwin would have a use for one . . . " Those were the times of gritted teeth. Up to then, I had taken pains to stress that I did love my children equally: duplicate sailor suits, duplicate bunk beds, duplicate toys. But with " . . . half a life" still ringing in my ears, and with five dollars per week between us and disaster, while we paid off debts to hospitals, to buy a useless bike for Erwin just did not make much sense.

I said that Christmas season: "Let's wait and buy him a bike when there's a chance that he will ride it."

"I won't have him cry on Christmas Eve," said Woldi and went out to order two beautiful bikes. The payment coupons came in the mail. I was left to pay them off with my household money.

Now I struggled with my demons. And the bike became a

symbol: just look at it and know that he won't ever make it on those wheels. That he won't ever make it on his own!

For years, it had been underfoot — wasted money, foolish hope, just sitting there, rusting away. Erwin showed no interest in his bike beyond an annoying insistence to "fix it" — translated, to take it apart. We argued over it a lot, Woldi and I. I wanted to sell it to recoup a few dollars; he wanted to hang on. When we left Canada, he took it along. "He'll learn to ride it yet," said Woldi, to have the last word. It lay, getting shabbier and rustier, in our cramped carport storage, and he would never ride it, and that, I told myself, was that!

I said to myself: "Even if I kill myself, will he make it on that bike?" Just what was I trying to prove? I came to dislike the bike's unholy presence, for in my mind it symbolized all the assorted terrors I now tried to pull to the fore: just what might happen to him, and to us, in just a few short years? Soon there would be manhood. Was there any point in going on?

"Why pretend?" I wanted to know. Why continue to hope for the day that might never come, no matter how we wished it? Did it not make sense to face up to reality?

"We went through all that yesterday," Woldi would reply.

No matter how often I tried to discuss it, Woldi would go into hiding. Woldi had a way of vanishing into passivity that set my teeth on edge. Woldi would develop headaches. He would duck behind a shrug, or a joke, or a sneer about my bookish wisdom.

"I love him," he would say, a righteous man, and thereby shame me into silence.

"I love him, too," I might or might not say. The child did ugly things to us. And yet, we all stood trapped.

There was a diagnostic clinic, an adjunct to the public school district's pupil services. As part of my training, I had begun to understand the rationale for testing theory, and I began to ask myself: just what was Erwin's "true" potential now that he had some language; what's more, now that he—we!—all spoke English fluently?

I called for an appointment to have him reassessed, thinking all the while defensively: "I already know that he is slow. So what if they tell me again?!"

Shortly thereafter, a sweet little lady knocked on my door: "I am the school psychologist . . . "

Once upon a time, psychologists had been my fiercest enemies, putting all the obstacles they knew into my path to bar my child from school. "How do you do?" I said, shaking her hand. "I'm studying to be one."

Her name, as I recall, was Edna. Edna took one look and told me briskly: "That kid belongs in public school."

I said, trembling in my nylons: "Edna, do you really think so, too?"

"Don't you?" she said, with raised eyebrows. "I've read about you in our bulletins . . . " Our glances locked. I was still active in a parent group that I had helped to launch, a "Midwest counterpart" to the Canadian ACLD. I was a pro, a fine and fervent asset. For a while, I had thrown myself into membership drives. I had helped with postage stamps. I had helped design pamphlets. I had helped organize workshops. Many times I had calmed a distraught parent on the telephone. I had done my part, and more, to spread the well-known gospel: differential diagnosis, modality training, individualized classes, sensory restructuring. Of late, I had been wearying. But when my instant friend, this Edna, said, " . . . well, little fellow. Don't you have the disease inflicted by the gods . . . ?" I knew: this is a feisty trooper from the trenches! I smelled the smell of battlefield again and cried: "By golly, Edna! Let's get going!"

She said: "Not every school will take him. I don't need to tell you that. But I have in mind one or two special education teachers I have spent years re-educating to the needs of special kids. Would you mind an awful lot driving him to Lincoln School? We'll reimburse you for your mileage . . . "

"Oh, Edna. Of course not. I'll gladly drive him to the moon . . . " Lincoln School was in the farthest southeast part of town. We lived in the farthest northwest. It meant three hours extra on the road, fighting heavy city traffic. But glory—did it matter?

"Well, you know the situation," said Edna, soberly. "You know that it's gonna be one step at a time . . . "

I looked at her. She looked at me. We were two pioneers. "It will work," said Edna, firmly. "He's obedient. He sits still. It's not just for his sake. It's for the sake of others. We've got to move 'em into public schools . . . "

One merry day, to diffuse a throbbing headache, I threw myself into aggressive housecleaning, and to that end, I called upon the help of a freelance carpet cleaner from the city's poorest neighborhood. I heard him trip and stumble over Erwin's bike as he unloaded his equipment. He had brought one of his sons along, a scroungy little boy with snapping eyes that just about popped out of their sockets when his father lifted the rusty contraption and, cussing heartily, kicked it to the side. I never saw such rapture in a small child's face.

"It's yours," I said, my heart a blob of lead. "Just take it away." I no longer wished to see that bike. I longed to lance the abscess.

No sooner did Erwin come home that day from his school than he cried in a voice thick with panic:

"Where's-my-bike-where-is-it-where?"

"I gave it away," I said. "Try to speak slowly."

"What-did-you-do-a-stupid-thing-like-stupid-thing-like-that-for?"

"Slow down. Slow down." The old recurring malady had surfaced once again. He jumbled and garbled his syntax.

"A-stupid-thing-like-that-what-for-did-you-a-stupid-thing-like-that-for?"

"It wasn't stupid, *Schatzi* . . . "

"My-very-own-bike!" he said, shuddering.

"Well," I said, bracing myself to the rest of my life, and his own. "You couldn't ride it, as you know. It was of no use to you."

"Just-about-to-ride-it-use-it-did-I-ride-it-just-about." Ten thousand injured tremors in his voice.

He was big now. He was lanky. In just a small handful of years, he would be a man. I pulled him down. Soon he would no longer let me hold him on my knees. I hugged him tightly to my chronic sorrow, gently rocking him.

"Listen hard, darling," I said. "You cannot ever ride a bike. I wish to God you could. When you were little, you hurt your head. You hurt it very badly. As a result, there are some things you simply cannot do. You cannot ride a bike. You can't. You can't. Not ever. Try hard to understand that."

The sun set on us both as we sat, cheek to cheek, facing darkness. " . . . I-was-just-about-to-learn-to-ride-and-understand-as-a-result . . . " he said softly.

I said, holding him and stroking him: "You can't. You can't, Erwin. If you could, I would buy you the shiniest bike in town. But I just know that you can't learn to ride a bike. Try to understand that."

"Try-to-understand-to-learn-to-ride-it-ride-it-ride-it . . . "

"I am sorry."

"Rudy's bike?" he said with yet another shudder. "The-shiniest-bike-in-town?"

A lump lay in my throat. Rudy had a right to his own life. Rudy had not had a childhood. Rudy's independence must count, too.

"No," I said. "Leave Rudy's bike alone."

Pearls of sweat sat on his face. "Help-me-Mom," he said, "to-push-the-shiniest-bike-in-town-to-ride-it-ride-it-ride-it . . . "

He fell.

I helped him to his feet.

He fell again.

He winced with anguish as I put a band-aid on his knee.

"Hurt-for-sure," he said, "as a result-to-ride-it-understand-it-shiniest-bike-in-town-to-me."

"Forget it, Erwin. Please. It is too hard for you."

"Push-me-as-a-result . . . "

I tried to hold his saddle for a while, but it was clear there was no use. If he must hurt, then he must hurt. The time had come for me to say: "I can no longer shelter you." I knew I must resolve to say, and not stand totally destroyed: "My child, I can no longer stand between you and your limitations. I do not serve you, or myself, if every time you hurt, I hurt. I am done with all that agony. I can't afford it any more." That's what it took. The will to say: You can't. You can't cross the street by yourself. You can't turn on the stove. You can't swim without supervision. You can't get your drivers' license. Or marry. Or have children. Some of life's deepest joys, my dearest son, will never be for you.

He sprained his toe. He bloodied his elbow. He tried. And tried. And tried.

We lived on a secluded street where it was safe for him to use the dead end. I watched him for a while, but when I heard the tuck-tuck-tuck of Woldi's car, I went inside and closed the door and blew my nose.

"Did you see that spunky kid?" cried Woldi, coming after me. "You know, I think that he's going to make it . . . "

"I can't believe it any more," I said, forcing the words past my restricted throat.

"Oh, he will," cried Woldi, enchanted. "And *you* wouldn't buy him that bike . . . "

I sat on the steps in the darkness. I said:

"In just a few more months, he will be a teenager. He still can't tie his shoes . . . "

Woldi said coldly: "Must you put poison into every moment . . . "

Nothing allied us. I had clawed my way out of my nightmare, alone. I had studied everything there was to study, and I knew there was no hope. Could I help it that four years of study of psychology now made me see a sharper truth? An abyss gaped between Erwin and children his age. It could only widen with the years.

I said:

"He'll soon be a man. And I will still . . . "

"I know. I know. You'll still wipe his behind. You told me fifty times already. So what!?"

"You're crazy . . . " I whispered.

"And you," said Woldi viciously, "you think you are so smart! You're crazy, that's what. You're loony. You're nuts. I've known that for years. Don't always blame the kid for all your emotional problems . . . "

In the darkness, I could hear Erwin's jumbled monologue. I said slowly: "I have given this much thought. I'm leaving you, Woldi. I can't live like this any more. Never seeing the end of the tunnel. Never having any time. Never having any money. Never having any semblance of security. What will become of me? Is it so wrong to debit life a little more in my behalf? I have a lot of talent. Am I so wicked, wanting to expand? I must find a way to re-direct my energies . . . "

"Go ahead. Go right ahead and use your fancy words on me . . . "

I said: "I had a birthday last week. I am now thirty-five years old. Half of my life is probably over. I haven't yet lived. Tomorrow, I'm taking my last set of exams. In all likelihood, my work will have earned me top honors. A *summa cum laude* degree. Do you know just what that means? Only three or four students, at most, from a class of over four hundred, will have accomplished what I will accomplish tomorrow. I love Erwin, too. I don't have to defend that. But he will always be an albatross around my neck, and I must find a way to carry him with lesser pain or perish . . . "

"You're just sore that I forgot your birthday," said Woldi, and slammed the door so hard that all the rafters shook.

Between exams, I struggled for breath in the restroom. I returned and tried again. The essay question swam before my eyes.

" . . . it has been claimed that adequate sensory experience is a prerequisite for normal development. A child must be able to see, hear, and feel objects in his environment correctly in order to acquire appropriate ways of responding. Please comment on deviant . . . "

I swallowed. I went on to the next:

" . . . learning has been defined as any relatively permanent change in behavior as a result of past experience. This definition excludes behavioral changes that take place in maturation, and also changes due to disease or physical damage. Explain 'bizarre' behavior in light of . . . "

Explain? I had lived it — for thirteen long years.

" . . . those individuals who have an IQ of 70 or less are regarded as mentally deficient. They are classified into three groups: morons, imbeciles, and idiots. Expand on this definition by outlining a behavioral differentiation chart in light of social functioning . . . "

I don't know what nonsense I wrote. I blew my *summa cum laude* degree. I lost it by one-hundredth of a point.

As I pulled out of the parking lot, I saw Paul coming down the stairs. He looked relieved that the semester was over. He sauntered in the sunshine — young and attractive, a little bored, a little spoiled, a little brash and snappy, now that the tedium was done. There walked a carefree man! This was the last time I would see him; my mission at the university was done. For four exhilarating years, I had fed off his fervor. I owed a world of inner wealth to him. I longed to tell him that, but how? He did look up. His grey, smart eyes went straight through me. I could tell that he did not know me any more. I was just another student, and another year was done, and by now he had forgotten me.

I slowed the car down a bit and watched him cross the street. I did not honk. I did not wave. I was too shaken and too shy to roll down my window and tell him goodbye.

Every tree leaf glistened as if sprayed with golden wax. I turned into our street, carefully keeping my foot near the brake pedal. It was a quiet deserted street, and children often toyed with danger on rollerskates or skateboards in the middle of the road. Sometimes they would, recklessly, race their bikes back and forth, and once or twice concerned citizens had called the police to warn them off the pavement. I saw one now, gyrating wildly, from afar a funny sight: a youngster in a striped pajama, hooting and waving and shouting, glasses dangling loosely from his nose.

"Watch out!!"

I swerved. I almost hit him with my car. It took me a second or two until the incredible registered. Why, wasn't that . . . wasn't that Erwin—cross-eyed, shins and elbows bloodied, drippy nose and all?

" . . . watch-me-Mommy-watch-the-shiniest-bike-in-town . . . !!"

I put my arms around my husband's neck and said: "You won. You won. I threw away my guns prematurely . . . "

With pencil in hand, I tried to re-map strategies. If Woldi was willing—why, so was I. With all my heart and all my strength and all my singleness of purpose I would try to be a wife and dedicated mother once again. I would relinquish all ambition. "If we want to keep this child," I told Woldi, "we must find a place where he fits in for life . . . " A small store, perhaps? A gas station? A modest motel? I would do all the paper work. Rudy would help with small errands. Erwin might perhaps change linens, or do garden work, or water the lawns. Once again, we would be a united family. I placed my finger on the State of California. A brand new start. In Sacramento. San Diego. Santa Barbara. Monterey.

"It's all the same to me," said Woldi, happier than I had seen him in years. "Pick your spot. Pick your place. What about this modest little town called Stockton . . . ?"

CHAPTER TWENTY SIX

A Kind of Death

L AST NIGHT I WEPT, remembering.
Ten years have passed since that day, eight years since we surrendered Erwin. Our lives were gutted in the fire of our child. Of the end I still can't speak. Yet from the very ashes came a new beginning.

THE LIFE OF ERWIN RIMLAND
by Erwin Rimland
May, 1979

I was born in Paraguay. I lived there for a while. Then I moved to Canada. Then I had a bad head injury and Rudy was born. Dad was a welder. Mother was taking care of us. I had a few friends. Then in 1967 we moved to the United States. There I started school. I walked a few blocks to school.

Then we moved to California. Dad worked at Valley Steel. Rudy started Junior High. Mom went to school. I started Eldorado School. Mrs. Busher was my teacher. Then I went to school in Lodi. Then I moved to a

Good Shepherd Home in El Toro, California. I was a little sad; I wanted to go back to Stockton.

I went to C.E. Utt in Tustin. Mrs. Terwillinger was my teacher. I went to school there for two years, and Rudy started High School. I had a great guy there; his name was Mr. Boyes. He and I had great times together. My folks got separated.

In 1975 I started El Toro High School. Mrs. Kelegian was my teacher. I had a lot of friends. My grades were good. My brother started driving. He went to Europe with Mother.

An idea is some kind of thought. A thought is an idea that came up. When I was little, I had a head injury. I couldn't remember anything so I went to school and got smarter. I am really not that handicapped. I think a lot, and I am smart. I have a hearing problem, and I got hearing aids. I can hear with them on. My brother had a few injuries, too. A slight head injury and an eye problem in Stockton, California, in 1971.

If I could wish for wishes to come true, I would wish for an apartment and a car to go to work. Some day my wishes might come true. Right now inventors are working on a device so I can do what I want to do.

I am 20 years old now. I graduated with honors. My Dad works in a shop. My Mom just got her doctor's degree. She is a book writer . . .

When we came to California, I despaired. It made no difference any more—I knew I could not rescue what could no longer be rescued. Even so, I tried:

"Look at this ad. Don't you think we ought to take the equity from our home . . . "

"A coffee shop in Lodi is for sale . . . "

"There is an empty plot right next to Highway 5 . . . "

Woldi built a swimming pool instead. Gone was the little money we had made by selling our Midwestern home.

I had to face it squarely. No one worked harder than Woldi, but Woldi, left alone, would never make it on his own. In all our years of marriage, never once had Woldi mailed a check. Never once had Woldi paid a bill. Every working day he carried his bologna sandwich in his old, scuffed lunch box, as he had done that first cold day in Canada, when we had been but kids, poor and shy, sad and confused, hoping that there was an answer for our bludgeoned baby in a rich and lavish land.

I saw one day that Woldi had turned grey. With his unassuming nature, with his utter lack of selfishness, Woldi would have served a lesser woman well, but I was different, I had changed. Across the gulf of years we looked at each other, now irrevocably strangers. I had almost completed my master's degree at the private University of the Pacific. My eyes were on a doctorate, thanks to assistantships and loans. I told myself that I was married to a man who could not even spell my name.

And, by our beautiful pool we could not afford and should not have built, I faced another truth. I had outgrown my quixotic emotional struggle. A decade and a half of fervor beat within me with the sounds of muffled drums. I still remembered, but all belief and sentiment had drained away from me. I had waited for years for a bad dream to end. Now I began to understand that I must end it, or it would stretch into my very grave. When Erwin was an infant, it often seemed he could not live. Now it occurred to me that he might well outlive me. What would become of him, once I was gone? Some hobo somewhere, part of the washed-up driftwood of life? No matter where I looked—a bleak gaping vacuum was there.

Once Erwin looked at me and said sadly: "I am a drag on you, huh?" He was very sweet and docile now. Adolescence brought a quiet, resigned demeanor. He would stand at the sidelines, gravely, watching younger children play. He tried hard not to be in anyone's way. "I am a total flop!" was written right across his face. The corners of his mouth would sag, but he would not complain. He just stood there, one scrappy bundle of mishap, quiet and sad beyond all words.

I would say to Woldi: "We've got to find him a life of his own."

"You wanted him in public school. He *is* in public school . . . " and Woldi's voice would crack. It was true: he was in public school; in fact, he was doing quite well. California was a proud, progressive state, a pioneer in special education. Not much hassle any more by anyone. Free testing. Free placement. Free transportation. True, his first school, Adams School, had kicked him out so fast we did not know what hit us, but then he found his niche at Eldorado School, and there he remained until it was time to move on, into a more advanced and "older" setting. They shipped him to a public school in Lodi, and then they said that he would have to go to Marshall Junior High. I was told that Marshall was a rowdy school, full of unwashed bodies, racial strife. I could not see my son at Marshall School. His strong medication had stunted his growth; he was half the size he should have been. He had a high and childish voice. He looked odd, to say the least, with his shuffling gait and squint and hearing aids and glasses. Immature and innocent and helpless, he would be a ready-made target to torment for someone with hurts of his own.

And there was Rudy, my forgotten child.

Never once did other youngsters Rudy's age come to our dark and joyless home. He did not have a single solid friend, it seemed, all through his teenage years. With Erwin he was patient. He held his hand to help him up the stairs. He built him little trinkets. He dressed him up for Halloween. I could hear them: Erwin's giddy giggle, Rudy's cautious " . . . watch it, now!" I remembered Rudy's tiny, furry head at birth, the shapely inked footprints, and I could have wept with loss. Soon Rudy would be grown, and I would never have a chance to know him as my own.

I would repeat: "We've got to find Erwin a home . . . "

Woldi would turn ashen and refuse to speak to me for days.

I looked at my calendar: My marriage endured another two years.

"An institution for your son?" Chuck Moody said, incredulous. Chuck Moody was a name someone had given me; he worked in some capacity for clients with developmental disabilities. The time had come for euphemisms. "Why, he is almost normal," said Chuck. "He reads. He writes. Don't you think he is quite independent . . . ?" At that, I put my face into my hands and fell into a pit.

Every once in a while, I still see Chuck's name in the paper. I doubt that he remembers me. He sat with me that day and spared me hollow platitudes and just pried Kleenex after soggy Kleenex from my fists.

"There is the Regional Center," he said in the end. "There is red tape, unfortunately. If you wish, I will come with you and help you make the application . . . " He will never know how much his silent understanding meant to me that autumn day in 1972 when I surrendered utterly.

In contrast to Chuck, the social worker who opened a "case" had other ideas.

"You need a lot of counseling," she told me briskly, living by a social worker's protocol. "To help you shed that heap of guilt."

I said I didn't need it; speed and efficiency would do. By then, I was steeped in all the latest theories of counseling. I could cite my statistics. The current literature was home to me. I said: "Please. Just don't make it difficult."

"Everyone needs counseling," declared the helpful soul. From behind her cluttered desk she eyed me severely. "Thinking it over," she called it. "Before we proceed . . . "

That extra year of stalling while she kept her big fat ass on Erwin's file to give me time to "think it over" was just enough to shatter my marriage beyond all repair.

In the end I walked into her office and declared: "I'll chain myself to the Governor's chair . . . " I knew she would react to that. The Regional Centers in California, dubious agencies at best as far as hurting parents were concerned, could not afford unfavorable press. Therefore, a lady was speedily summoned—a pimply, inexperienced, flustery thing. I could tell she was unqualified. She did not know her testing instruments at all. She started. I watched. She butchered the job. I told her I could help; I was a trained and duly certified psychologist. "Why don't you t . . . t . . . test him yourself?" she quavered.

Thus, hemlock came to me. I proved to local, state, and federal agencies that Subject Erwin Rimland was indeed retarded, in need of sheltered placement, with limited prognosis—as far as anyone could say, beyond all human help.

There is a special light in California nine months out of the year. The sky is transparent, the mornings are scented, the days are soft and lovely. But dark and chilly are the winters in the Valley.

A fog creeps in around the holidays. It is so thick you cannot see your feet. It seems that it will never lift, not in ten thousand lifetimes. Through that fog, through grey, ragged patches of fog, I drove alone five hundred miles to visit the Good Shepherd Lutheran Home of the West. Its newest branch, one out of seven or eight such homes designed to care for the retarded, was opening for registration in El Toro. Shiny with paint and smelling of new furniture, it seemed a place whose memory I could endure. It was, in fact, quite a beautiful complex: all brick, all tiles, in the middle of a lively, rich community in Orange County, one of the richest counties in the world. Three wings spread out to separate the residents according to their level of development and needs. There was a pool. There were long, sweeping sidewalks. There would be ample money in the surrounding public schools.

I should act fast, I was informed. The waiting list was long. A place like that, sheer luxury with no more than three beds per room, would fill up in no time at all.

Here is a letter from Erwin, dated a week after admission:

Dear Mother:

This is Erwin Rimland. How is Dad? How is my brother Rudy? I have a boy named Mitchell who sleeps with me. He wears a helmet. He is about 15 years of age, and he is my best friend. The only problem he has he can't talk, but he can write notes.

I have to go to a Christmas show on Saturday at 11:30 and another Christmas show on Saturday night at 7:00. I eat breakfast, lunch, and dinner in the kitchen. I made a table at workshop. I got it painted today. It is red. I am going to camp in the mountains next week. It was raining this afternoon. I went swimming down here. My roommate got a tape recorder. I had a sore throat last week, but I am better now. Mom, my watch is showing the wrong time.

Love, Erwin.

P.S. See you soon. Love, Erwin.

When our child left us for good, it was as though he had

never existed. Not a friend, not a neighbor said a word. At home, Woldi and I sat in griefstricken silence. I don't know what Rudy did. Christmas was upon us, loud and garish, obscene colors, obscene songs.

One late afternoon, I had to go to the university to pick up some papers, and on the steps I met a friend. I had known for some time that this man was fond of me for my "differentness." Once he had told me: "There is something very honest and straightforward and almost savage about you . . . " and I had known exactly what he meant.

Now we exchanged a few holiday greetings, and he invited me into his office. I knew that his marriage, too, was on the rocks. I sat with him and helped him wrap some presents for his children, and saw that his face was closed and in thought. Yet I could read them easily. I put my finger to his bows and showed him how to make sharp corners with the gold-and-silver Christmas foil while carols drifted through the radio. The wind threw grey against the window. Lumps of moisture kept on dripping from the roof. Rivers of tears sloshed into the gutters.

"You are hurting," this man said, suddenly putting a very warm hand over mine, and I leaned forward and into his arms. I knew he was a ladies' man, that he was not the man for me, and in the end he caused me suffering I did not need and could have done without. But that dark and foggy afternoon I slumped against him from the knowledge that three simple words regarding Erwin, offered up in casual sympathy, were the only words of understanding that anyone had ever said to me.

CHAPTER TWENTY SEVEN

The Wanderers

I TOOK AN APARTMENT two blocks down the road. I told Woldi: "I must be alone. I don't know how long it will take. It might be a month. A year. A lifetime. I really do not know. I only know I need to be alone."

I left him with 83 cents in my purse. With it, I bought three postage stamps to send out three job applications. With what was left, I bought a tiny pot of violets. I put those in my window.

My good friend Marta, a fellow doctoral student, came over that night to offer support. I did not have a chair to offer her. She sat with me on the carpet and toasted me with orange juice and told me she was on my side.

Dear Mom and Dad and Rudy:

I am very happy here. Mom, I got that Christmas present December 24th. I found it in the office. How many days will I stay here? Mom, I got that clock for Christmas, but the battery in the clock doesn't work . . .

It was strange: the struggle was over, the poison was gone. There was no longer any need to fight. Woldi and I became ever so gentle and kind with each other. We spoke in hushed tones as if someone whom we loved had died and we must do our share of grieving, but we knew that it was almost done. Already we could sit and talk, tattered battle friends, within a grey and gentle peace. The constant irritant was gone.

I told him I would keep my separate place for as long as I needed to finish my Mennonite novel. I had spread my manuscript all over three small empty rooms. I had found a publisher. Once and for all, I would be free to say what I had always longed to say.

I found part-time work in a neighboring city—just enough to pay my bills. After work each day, I spent a few hours with Rudy. I set my routine: An early riser anyway, I would awake at five o'clock, drive "home" from my apartment to knock on Woldi's door, sit with him and share a steaming cup of coffee before he left for work, wake Rudy and give him his breakfast, and then, refreshed, take off for work. The knot within my stomach had dissolved. My hands stopped shaking. My skin cleared up. My palpitations disappeared. I told Woldi that I was amazed at how good and tranquil life could be.

One day, I don't remember when, I told him I was strong enough to try once more—to give us both a chance. I said I was not sure that it would last. I said I knew that I had hurt him very badly. I said I was willing to shoulder my share of the blame. I missed my home. I worried about Rudy.

Woldi looked ever so pleased.

"OK," Woldi said, and I could see that he would say no more. My aberration was settled—I could see that he felt smug that I had settled it. He picked up a rock to graze a neighbor's cat that was venturing too close and deftly changed the subject. I had to smile at him. What had I expected? That he would take me out? That he would buy me those proverbial long-stemmed roses? Perhaps an offer to help me move some of the furniture I had acquired this past year?

That weekend he went fishing. He came back late Sunday night, having caught a trout which he held up by a gigantic fin and I admired duly. He smoked it, whistling, in the back yard, next to our shimmering pool. I sat nearby and had a beer with him and talked to him and then went peacefully to sleep, alone, in my apartment. He plain forgot to ask why I had changed my mind.

To Mother:

I love you, Mother. I love to write you a Mother's Day card. I like my teacher and my friends. I wanted to write you a greeting. Love, Erwin.

(inside a primitive drawing: Superman flying over a home)

I think back with warmth on my years of full time service as a psychologist in public schools. I served four schools, close to two thousand children, close to a hundred teachers who all respected, loved, and appreciated me. No matter what I touched, it turned out well. For so long, I had fought the schools from without. Now I was part and parcel of their strengths and limitations.

I now understood from a much different perspective that there was no way that Erwin could have functioned as he did "within the system" in his young, torrential years. The teachers at that time had no tools, no training, no knowledge to handle a child such as mine. In all my years of practice, I have never come across a child who hurt as much as Erwin did when he was growing up. But things were changing now. There was more money. There was more willingness. And then, in 1975, there was a comprehensive, sweeping law—henceforth, in the United

States, from sea to shining sea, no child could be denied an education due to severity of handicap.

I bought a new car. I furnished my apartment. I bought a lot next to the university and planned to build a house. Since I was still a married woman and hence suspect for wanting a place of my own, I was denied bank credit and had to abandon my plans. But I remembered a friend in the real estate business, bought him a drink and twisted his arm, and managed to purchase a smaller but pretty, sunflooded condo.

I took my one remaining son to live with me. I took Rudy to Spokane, Washington, to the World's Fair, to Vancouver, later on to Europe. For the first time in my life, I had a little extra money. I could afford some luxuries: pretty clothes, pretty haircuts, pretty shoes. I entered the doctoral program. I made a name for myself in the Valley. I eagerly finished my book.

In 1977, my Mennonite novel was published. It was, from the start, a bombshell success.

I am inordinately proud of that book, not just for what it says, but for my focused voice and strong conviction within the circumstances and the stresses in which I wrote my version of what needed to be said regarding Mennonites: who they are, where they come from, what made them what they are today. In my vainer moments, I am convinced the Mennonites don't have a better book. They have said as much, at their schools and colleges, in their many churches up and down this glorious land where they invited me and where I told them, at their invitation, why I thought and why I wrote the way I did. *The Wanderers* is my artistic explanation mark for the historic forces that brought me where I am today: a thinking, independent person with a rich and varied ethnic past and a deeper understanding of the evil things that come to us: not out of malice but from ignorance.

Young Mennonites in the United States and Canada agree:

they follow me around, they say I speak for them, they see themselves and their own struggles within the mirror of my book. The young say they adore me. One or two oldsters aren't so sure.

The Wanderers changed my direction. It gave me a focus for the rest of my life. It won the highest award for fiction given to a California writer for that year, the California Literature Medal Award, and at the ceremony in the Gold Room at the posh Fairmont Hotel in fabled San Francisco, no one less than Alex Haley was the luncheon speaker. I had him autograph my check book for good luck. There were flashbulbs. Cameras. There were glowing book reviews all over the United States and Canada. There were tours. Parties. Speaking engagements. There were radio and TV. There were thousands of letters from readers. There was, plain and simple, everywhere I turned and looked, sweet and heady victory.

"What's all this ruckus about?" my almost-ex-husband wanted to know.

"Well, it seems that I have made it. It seems I have become a star."

"No kidding." Genuine gladness. "Can I read it?"

Nonchalantly: "Sure. Of course."

I was dying to have him read it. Surely he of all people would finally begin to understand just who I was, all this long and unarticulated time, just what I tried to do. I gave him his very own copy. I placed it first, kind of casually, on top of his refrigerator, next to his brand new fancy tackle box. There it remained. Untouched. I put it on the counter. I moved it to his night stand. Nothing. Zilch.

In the end, I could not stand it any more. I said: "Well, aren't you going to read it?"

"I started. But frankly, it's kind of hard to read . . . "

"What do you mean?"

"Well, to tell the truth, it's kind of boring . . . "

Howl. "It's an acclaimed, award-winning book!!! I can't believe my ears!!!"

"Well, for other people perhaps," amended my good love of almost thirty years. "I can see that they might want to read it. But what could you possibly tell me that I haven't heard all my life . . . ?"

So much for the prophet within his own house. He never has read it, to this very day. But he proudly bought a dozen copies, at family discount, to disperse among his relatives and friends.

CHAPTER TWENTY EIGHT

Letters from Erwin

. . . Dear Mom and Dad:
How is my dear Rudy? I am having a party tonight at my new home. Someone gave me a ride to Sunday School yesterday morning, and I won't find a school to go to until after Christmas. How are you, Mother? I am fine. I work at the Unit on Saturdays. I see you all on January 27th, at 3:30 in the afternoon . . .

. . . Dear Mother:
I was very surprised to see you on Saturday. Did you have a safe trip back to Stockton? Yesterday, I washed two cars and went out for a doughnut. Did you all like the story that I typed? Is Dad's car out of the shop yet? I worked very hard at the workshop today. I am going to camp soon. Let me know when Dad is moving to the new house. I want you to give this picture to Rudy to remind him of me. Write to me. Love, Erwin . . .

. . . Dear Mother:
Here is the list of things I want for my birthday: 1)

Walkie Talkie 2) Books 3) Model Car 4) Puzzle 5) Smashup Debbie 6) Bionic Man 7) Love, Erwin . . .

. . . Dear Dad:
Thank you for inviting me over to your house for Christmas vacation. I liked that goose you made for Christmas dinner. Also, I like that old train you showed me. Thank you for driving me back to Good Shepherd . . .

. . . Dear Rudy:
How are you? I am fine. I am doing fine in school. How are you doing in school? I will be going to night school next year. What have you been up to? Are you still riding your bike to school? I went to a party last night. This week we have two new kids in the classroom. We have a boy and a girl. They are nice to me. Hope to see you in February. Oh, Mom! I have a new teacher; her name is Mrs. Kay. She is nice. Mrs. Terwillinger is sick for a while. I went to the movies Sunday night. I got back about 10:00. How are you all? Rudy, I know your birthday is next week. Is my mother happy . . . ?

. . . Dear Mrs. Ingrid Rimland:
I made you a rubber stamp to stamp on paper with ink. Love, Erwin . . .

. . . Dear Mom:
I had fun flying in the air all by myself. Hope Dad will get me a watch for my birthday. How is Rudy? I was on a field trip Friday, and I did like the field trip. My bike still works. Hope to see you all sometime in the summer. Dad, how are you doing? Dianne picked me up at the Orange County Airport. I am happy to be here.
Love, Erwin . . .

. . . Dear Mother:
I love you, Mom, because you are my best friend
when I am lonely, and you are important to me.
Thank you for taking me shopping . . .

He had bled my life from me, and I wanted to forget him. I
had surrendered him, and I did not want to live in chains any
more. I looked out for his welfare, and I flew him home at inter-
vals, but I no longer wished to be involved. I kept my contacts
with home and school personnel formal and sparse. The am-
putation had been done. Never again would I be whole, but the
excruciating pain was gone. I was healing finally. I wanted to be
left alone; I wanted to live and let live.

But his sweet little missives kept tumbling in my mail drop.
They kept tugging at my heart.

I received a little clipping in the mail, an excerpt from the
junior high school paper. There was a drawing, a cartoon, of a
student carrying a sign: "Erwin for Principal." Underneath the
caption was a mock "celebrity interview:"

Mr. Stepnitz, our principal here at C.E. Utt, now
has competition with Erwin Rimland for the top job.
Erwin loves school so much that he would like to
grow up to be a principal.

Erwin was born in Paraguay, South America, on
May 5th 1959, and now lives at the Good Shepherd
Home of the West, along with 101 other people. His
parents were born in Russia, and his brother in
Canada.

In Erwin's spare time, he likes to watch Speed
Racer with his roommate, Mike Allen. His spare time
at school is spent in Graphic Arts, which he enjoys
very much. He loves to read, and does all the time.
Mystery books and nursery rhymes rate the best type

of books, according to him. His favorite magazine is Sports Life.

At the Good Shepherd Home, he enjoys their pets. His favorites are a pony and a white dog called Goldie.

Erwin's fellow students and friends are Paul, Mike, Chris, Greg, Denise, Diane, and Janet.

HAPPY BIRTHDAY, ERWIN!!!

His teacher wanted to know: could I possibly come? Erwin seemed to think that this time I would come to help him celebrate his sixteenth birthday.

My heart was heavy, driving through the valley. I realized I dreaded seeing him — an abandoned freak among a bunch of normal children. What would I find? I sat there at Denny's for the longest of time, staring into my coffee. Now that I worked in public schools, I knew from my own experience that brand of teenage cruelty that could lodge on junior high school campuses. Would they tease my poor, defenseless child? Would they trip him? Push him? Call him names?

I had bought a little nightstand radio for a present. I pulled into the parking lot. I parked my car, clutched my beribboned package to my thumping heart, and stepped with gritted teeth into a pothole. The school custodian stopped his raking leaves, smiled beamingly at me, and cried: "Hello there! Good morning, Mrs. Rimland . . . "

Now that was odd. How did he know my name?

I walked along the sidewalk. Two teenagers, sitting in the grass, jumped up and said: "Hi, Mrs. Rimland."

"Hello," I said, bewildered.

"This way," said one. Three or four others joined in. I was growing a tail. More and more followed. From everywhere, teenagers joined, teenagers followed. Everywhere youngsters smiled, youngsters waved. I opened the door to the office, and the secretary shot from her seat like a rocket released and grabbed my hand and shook it mightily, exclaiming: "Why, there you are! There you are! We were afraid you wouldn't make it . . . !" The principal appeared to pump my arm as well: "Well, there you are! There you are! Well, and all this time . . . well, durnit! How 'bout that . . . !"

The teacher said: "He is our mascot."

She said: "If one should push him down, ten would stand up for him . . . "

She said: "The other day, we found the school's worst bully hiding in a closet, repairing Erwin's lunch kit . . . "

It may be trite, but it's the truth: I realized that when I let him go, he came into his own.

CHAPTER TWENTY NINE

New Friends

MANY OF MY GOOD FRIENDS want to know: given all my trials and tribulations — well, what about the Lord? Did the Lord not come to me? What a lovely story that would make, and what a neat and clear-cut ending. It would also sell 300,000 extra copies of this book. I would be rich, and I could then recline in comfort and serenity and would not have to earn my keep while worrying about the pioneering work that still piles up on me.

I must stick to my own brand of honesty and report that He, alas, has not as yet found me. I believe the good Lord has it up His sleeve to knock on this contrite sinner's door when all the work in public schools is done, when our little misfits drifting in and out of special classes no longer need a firebrand like me.

We now have acceptance and money and space, but we still lack instructional techniques. Nobody really knows just how to teach our little less-than-perfect minds differentially. Also, there's much too much sorting and sifting. Special education has become a dumping ground for all that's wrong in our schools; we have in our special classes not only learning but all too many teaching-disabled children. Now and then we change our labels, but the problems do not change. There is still a lot of mileage to be covered, and guess who tries to cover it?

I wish it were different, but what can I do? So I putter along, with consultancy work for five or six surrounding school districts, in my private practice where brand new parents bring me brand new worries every day, and in my publications where I can speak my mind and do my part to influence the thrust of education. In my darker moments, I still quarrel with the Lord: "That was a lot of punishment for just a little sin!" I do not get an answer. It always seems He speaks to others much more clearly than to me.

But here is a concession: I must admit that lately I have quarreled less.

Here's why.

It looks to me as if circle after circle in my life has closed with meaning, and it looks as if there is a higher order and consistency for which I can't take credit by myself. One little child was hurt—yet thousands upon thousands have been helped. When I first wrote this statement, my editor and dearest soulmate Betty Lou, a special parent and seasoned pioneer herself, said cautiously: "Don't you think you better take that out? Or tone it down? You didn't do it by yourself, you know . . . "

Of course I didn't do it by myself—other parents fought as I fought, against all the odds in the world. It was a struggle singularly lonely, for each and every one of us, difficult beyond all words. Those who work in special education now take many things for granted. Not us—that small handful of militant parents who, less than two decades ago, rolled that first boulder of heartache uphill. I say today, as many others do: "Your children wouldn't be in public school had it not been for our belief and fortitude and stubborn strength and missionary zeal . . . "

My life has been hard. It has also been rich beyond measure. I have been in the pits—I have climbed to the top. I had no schools when I was young—now I am guiding teachers. I fought the Mennonites with all I had for their supposed narrowness—today I am required reading in their colleges. Old conflicts have been laid to rest. Door after door has been opened. I had no life for half my life — now I can see that what is left of life can still be good and, in rare moments, stunning.

One of the many parents who have written to me over the years tried to put this into words: "There is a real mix in life — a mix of suffering, pain, joy and success. For Christians, this mix is not accidental . . . " Two years ago, this father lost a son. Now he quoted M. Scott Peck from *The Road Less Travelled:* "Life is difficult. This is a great truth, one of the greatest truths. It is a great truth, because once we truly see this truth, we transcend it. Because it is accepted, the fact that life is difficult no longer matters . . . " My heart is still sore; I'm not at all sure I agree. But I know what this grieving parent tries to tell me. I have been there. My entire being knows that suffering helps us to grasp the depth of life, and death, more richly and more firmly.

My hero Paul, young and arrogant and carefree, in the end was singled out to learn this lesson, too, and my heart goes out to him for the circumstances. His younger son, four years of age, coasted backwards on a tricycle into the path of a brute car. The fatal accident changed Paul — the former youthful radical became a serious Christian. Those who knew him shook their heads: It would not last. It did.

I met him again on one of my tours on behalf of my novel. For here is yet another circle providence completed. I returned to my *alma mater* as their proud alumna, coinciding with the Fifteenth Mennonite World Conference that was held in the very city where, not all that long ago, I stood at the steps of a university, awash with incoherence. Not only could I claim to be a Mennonite of sorts, I was a sort of "city" girl: here I had earned my scholarships, here I had first learned English, here my child had started school. We both made good. My picture and my story were displayed in every paper. My voice was heard on every radio and TV.

Paul must have heard of me; he must have remembered. He sat in on one of my presentations. He sat in the very first row, a tall, slightly stooped, middle-aged man. I noticed him tangentially for his intense expression, but I did not recognize him any more. Ten years had passed. The mentor who had set me on the path of knowledge and success had changed beyond reclaim.

Paul says the good Lord fixed it so he and I could meet, alone, in a little coffee shop. There I talked to him, friend to equal friend, as I have seldom talked to anyone. Grief has a way of welding in a hurry. I will never forget that quiet, sad, poignant little encounter in that little restaurant. When we said goodbye, Paul briefly put his face to mine and said: "Ingrid, I love you."

I said: "I love you, too."

Some people live and die and never know a perfect moment. I cherish mine forever in my heart.

When I write of glimpses of great poignancy, I find it difficult to translate all the sweetness that, in recent years, has found its way to me. When I was young and self-absorbed and hurting, I was very much alone, but maturity and distance from my struggle have brought dear and valued friends. I have many close and loyal friends whom I cherish. My story would be incomplete, were they not included in this book.

There's Jaroslav Vajda who published my novel and in the process fell a little bit in love with me. There's Walter and his wife, Antoinette, whom I met in the Midwest and who, when it seemed that The Academy would confiscate my roof, offered to sign over every spoon they owned as collateral for me. There was Dan, a NASA scientist and the most prolific letter writer I have ever known, and Jack, a brilliant conversationalist who fed me oysters and champagne when I confided that, thanks to divorce, I did not have a nickel to my name.

There was Jerry, who taught me all the ins and outs of navigating in our schools when I was just a neophyte and scared to death to tackle the problems of two thousand children all at once. There are Nancy, Marta, Inge—fellow school psychologists and supergals. There's my childhood chum Elvira, who lives in Santa Barbara, the only Mennonite who closed her ears and set her jaw and stuck it out with me. Elvira is closer to me than a sister. There's Charlotte in Carlsbad, who has given me the finest little parties with select and comfortable friends to help me make it through the blues. There are Al and Jane and Bill who, only recently, taxied up their private airplane and whisked me off to the Bahamas for a spectacular vacation, just to see me through this book. I have many writer friends in California and surroundings who love me without reservation, in whose eyes I do no wrong.

And I guess there's Woldi as well. He still checks my car. I still do his income tax returns. The other day he called me in great panic. He had to sign some papers for a retirement transaction, and what was he to do? "It says here: 'Marital status.' What do I put down?"

I said: "You're divorced. You have been divorced for over a year."

"Oh." Long pause. "Then why do you still have my name?"

"If you don't mind," I told him gently, "I would like to keep it. As a souvenir."

Yes, I have friends, and there are more to come. I have on my careful list of friends-yet-to-be-made the following encircled as priorities: William Buckley, Jr., Barbara Walters, Edwin Newman, Shana Alexander, Phil Donahue, Joan Didion, Melvin Belli, and Herb Caen. And the day I manage to have lunch with Eric Sevareid, the man who uses words like polished swords, I'm sure I'll fold my wings around myself and die of blessed rapture.

And last but not least, there's a brand new friend that I am proud to call my own—a sweet and classy lady, Ann Landers.

You see, for emulation's sake, in time I too became a columnist. One day I opened the *Record*, and what did I see? There we were, side by side, my old reliable ally and I. My memory wheel spun back—not all that long ago, I had learned to sharpen my tongue on behalf of my child on her smart and chatty wit, and here we met again: the same space, the same layout, columnist smile facing columnist smile. I sat down and wrote her a blurry-eyed letter. Within three days I had a reply.

We met last year in Anaheim, where she had come for a speaking engagement, and afterwards I packed her in my car and drove her all the way to Hollywood. I told her where I had been, how far I had come, where I was going, and why. I said to her: "Before I die, I'll get me a Pulitzer yet." She said: "I don't doubt that for a moment." For that, she will get the first copy, hand-delivered to her door. You would never know it from her sassy column, but Ann Landers is quite shy. Now she rummaged through her purse and dug up a little pin—a polka-dotted ladybug.

"For good luck," said Ann Landers, America's umpire. "You wear this for good luck."

Just watch me!

To finish this book with appropriate flair, I might as well tell about Claude. He taught me, more than anybody else, just how profoundly I've been altered in my nature by my child.

I met Claude several years ago on a blind date at the lovely Mansion Inn in Sacramento while, upstairs, the California Writers Club helped celebrate my book.

He was a graceful, gracious man, erudite and worldly. You know how you know? I just knew. My entire being stood on tip-toe. Not a cell in my body was in doubt. I said to him: "I have just gotten word of my award. Will you come with me and stay with me and be my love?"

I wrote a book around his answer. I never sold it, though.

I flooded him with loving missives when he moved East and I stayed West. I wrote him every week, a gratifying ritual that took my silent, introspective Sunday mornings for some four growing years.

In-between, he married and divorced.

"For years," he wrote me, none the worse for wear and tear, "I have carried around with me the image of a perfect woman. She has been nameless and faceless, but every nuance of her soul has been apparent to me. You have emerged from the shadows to give substance to my reveries. You are my total woman—cerebral yet not overwhelmingly, assertive yet not dogmatic, proud and self-possessed yet vulnerable, scholarly disciplined yet evoking powerful rhythms of sensuality. You must have a glorious and radiant soul—I can feel its warmth encompass me . . . "

Can you believe it? What woman would not have been mesmerized? Ingrid was bewitched.

I met him again about two years ago in Washington, D.C.

He said: "Why me?"

I said: "You have such impeccable manners. You are so suave. You are so polished. May I take you out on loan?"

He drove me to New York where I was to meet with renowned executive powers on Publishers Row to discuss a budding book or two.

I said to Claude: "Will you please watch me and rescue me if needed . . . ?"

And my Claude did me proud. You know the Russian Tea Room in New York where bestselling authors and such congregate? That's where we met Grace Bechtold, no doubt one of the world's savviest editors. There, for posterity's record, we lunched in elegance and splendor, with *Bantam* picking up the tab. Claude conversed with silver tongue. Grace, sixtyish or so, giggled like a teenager. Claude lit cigarette after cigarette for her with the smoothest gestures I have ever seen. Claude moved her chair. Claude wrapped her in her mink coat. Claude held her arm, a smashing cavalier. I trod behind, a peasant.

In the end, Grace fixed a benevolent eye on me and said wistfully: "A sequel to *The Wanderers,* yes. There's good potential there. Write me some fifty pages, and I will let you know. But the market is flooded with stories of defective children. The market just won't take these stories any more . . . "

So much for that.

Claude, to deflect defeat, hugged me to his warm and furry sweater: "By the minute, you become more glamorous . . . "

For good measure Claude, a devout Catholic, took me to St. Patrick's Cathedral to say an appropriate prayer to an appropriate saint and light a small candle to hurry up success. I have never been so touched in all my life.

He kissed me somewhere in New Jersey: "Could it be that I'm falling in love . . . ?"

In Washington, he promenaded me, my clammy hand in his, right past the White House, and I ran my fingertips across its ornamental fences and saw the mudhuts of my youth.

By romantic candlelight Claude said: "My dear, I'm just a lightweight. You have lots and lots of weight, and I am just a lightweight."

You know how you know? At that moment I knew. He needed a playmate. I needed a mate. I had solidified. I could no longer toy at love. And so he paid my tab and took my arm and we drove home in silence.

Shortly afterwards, he sat with me on a porch in Alexandria, Virginia. He said: "I am involved with this kid . . . "

His "Lolita," he explained to me, was a thirty-year-old, not-too-swift beauty parlor operator—a gal who had been beaten up by previous husbands and whom he now took pleasure squiring around town.

"She calls me Mr. Wonderful," said Claude.

Thus spake Claude in whose path, in my sundry jealous torments, all the elegant ladies of Washington swooned. His lips toyed with my fingertips. I stroked his knee. Here was a belated lesson. When I was thirty, I was ancient. Claude, my love, was fifty-five. He was right. I was lead. He wanted fluff. Ingrid was aghast.

As I was finishing this book and struggling to translate this transitory interlude, there was a barrage of objections from friends: Claude did not belong in this book. I was to cut him out and write him off and get on with the business of writing my usual substantive stories.

Well, they are wrong. Claude was part of an end and a beginning for me; he was part of savoring the mystery of love that only brushed me briefly. That was the year when I began to know that there was life after Erwin. There was even life after Claude. To this day, my memories marked "Claude" can soften me to beauty. I hold those memories in awe. Claude and I share secrets that could never be translated for consumption, that are kept where only rare and precious gems are kept.

It was a sweet and fragile thing while it lasted. Why did it not work out? Search me! For a while, I walked the streets of Washington in agony, but all the while I knew. And so I walked away.

Now we write gentle, faintly distant missives to each other. When I see his swanky letters on that envelope I recognize at once, I pause and savor it — still, all in all, a moment of caress. And then I think, to have the last laugh in this matter: "Well, what do *you* know? Given my tenacity, I know — as you can't know! — that we still have a date with destiny . . . "

CHAPTER THIRTY

Five Seconds

I SIT HERE, FINISHING this book, Erwin's yearbooks in my lap, and I hear many voices:

"... everyone at El Toro High will remember you for all the happiness you brought to our school. Much love from your teacher ... "

"... Whatever am I going to do here without such a friendly person greeting me every day? You are a very special person to me. I will miss you and your great love and kindness to everyone. Good luck to a great individual. Remember me as your buddy ... "

"... Have a nice summer and stay cool ... "

"... you are one of my best friends ... " "... I'll miss you ... " "... It was fun having you at our school ... " "... It was great having you ... " "... have a good time this summer ... " "... your friend always ... " "... you're a great guy. Stay that way ... " "... Erwin, you're my buddy." "... good luck always ... " "... you are real nice ... " "... Happy grad, and good luck ... "

One had written: "... Erwin, this is the entire secret of knowledge: $E = mc^2$. You can manage that ... "

Who is to say? He may have managed that, and more. It was a struggle lasting more than twenty years, and in the end, five seconds were given to me in exchange.

" . . . Diane Morris . . . "

" . . . Cynthia Parker . . . "

" . . . Erwin Rimland . . . "

I see him step forward to receive his public high school diploma. Rare are the moments in life that pierce you with perfection. A strong stir passes through the audience. Applause. More applause. Applause from all over the field. It swells and swells. Hundreds, apparently, know him. A mother's heart will count: Two seconds. Three. Four. Five. He stands, small and smiling, in the middle of the giant football field, yellow honors' tassle moving softly in the breeze.

" . . . Gregory Roberts . . . " calls the announcer, and Erwin steps back into line.

I sit far away. Have I been right in my push for those seconds? Have I been wrong? I threw my life behind my child, and found I could not live. Then, to survive, I distanced myself, and found I did not die. This child of mine put me in a thousand chains, yet through my very limitations I helped bring a richer life to others. Somewhere someone said: "Moments of true peace come rarely in the lives of parents of handicapped children. Perhaps we can no longer feel them when they come." I clutch onto my moment now. He marked my life with such severity, and yet, would I have truly ever been enriched as I am now? Five seconds, too, are part of God's eternity—just long enough to strike a match to an eternal flame.

" . . . Susan Ryan . . . "

" . . . Peter Stivers . . . "

I borrow a saying: Take what you want, said God, and pay for it. I did both, in fullest measure. And to what end? What is the balance? Nil? Or priceless? If he is almost blind, what does that mean? If there are stares of pity, he cannot see them. What if he cannot hear? He can shut off vexation. What if he cannot walk through life as you and I? Let time fly by, let him stand still—nobody I know savors time more deeply. What if his wires cross? He is not wired to experience hate, dissatisfaction, greed. He cannot even tell a lie, for doing so would shatter his small grasp on what is true and what is not, and so he speaks the truth in innocence. He, forever young, has robbed me of my youth and possibilities, yet a ballad should be sung to him; his name should shine in gilded letters.

For he has learned to read and write. He can spell, not only forwards but backwards. "Watch me," his words play in my ears, a fine and long-remembered melody, "I'll get me a mountainseed. I'll grow me my very own mountain . . . " What if our rules do not apply to him? Who is to say his garbled rules don't count? The little heart that twenty years ago was jumped with some galvanic batteries is very wide indeed.

" . . . Craig Takata . . . "

" . . . Lisa Walker . . . "

I listen to these names of pride and honor as all those years roll by. For two decades, I lived from crisis to crisis. Life is short. Years come and go. Where will all these youngsters be—ten, twenty years from now? They seem so willing, idealistic, pliable—their future seems awash with laughter and with promise. The kiln of suffering has made me hard. What will life teach them in the end?

"We learn lessons from affliction," all religions in the world proclaim, but do we? Do we really? Is that statement even true, much less its easy promise? What did I learn—what have I gained? The focus of my intellect? My stubborn strength of character? The sweet ability to touch another heart with words? I would trade you all that—in a minute!—if I could savor just a glimpse of Erwin as he should have been, as he will never be. And yet, those were not empty years. Perhaps this is my lesson: To know that sorrow comes, ever again, in great lapping waves to wash away the sediment of trivia. What's left is this: a sense of who I was, or should have been, or might become. And why.

" . . . Cory Wilson . . . "

Tomorrow I'll go home, alone. I'll drive through hills no longer wrapped in fog, for it is June, and sky and earth are hot and clear. To the left, along the coast, lie mountain chains in all their California fragrance. I know that somewhere in the universe there exists a mountainseed, just as a unicorn exists, or a dream, or a love song, or an individual snowflake not duplicated anywhere in all the myriad snowflakes in the world.

I know it does, for there are miracles. The ocean air begins to wash my face, and I begin to know that I am free.

"Walter York . . . "

Their caps fly in the air. These youngsters here will scatter — new ones will fill the desks and benches left behind. I know that I have forged a better world for many other children — now welcome in public schools, too. The generation of today is gentle and patient with lesser minds than theirs. They love my son. Erwin stands surrounded by a thick, chatty cluster — a tousled speck of hard-won self-control and discipline among our finest and our best. He wears an honors tassel, just as they. They bend to him. They hug him and they kiss him. One of them says tenderly: "Honey, you can come with me. I'll help you change your gown." Her golden hair falls over Erwin's happy face. She looks elegant. She looks smart and strong and generous and beautiful. She is young, as I was young just yesterday.